JACKS FORK

BOOKS BY CHRIS ORLET

In the Pines
A Taste of Shotgun
So Many Things To Bury
Jacks Fork

CHRIS ORLET

JACKS FORK

Copyright © 2025 by Chris Orlet

All rights reserved. No part of the book may be reproduced in any form or by any electronic or mechanical means, including information storage and retrieval systems, without permission in writing from the publisher, except by a reviewer who may quote brief passages in a review. Without in any way limiting the author's [and publisher's] exclusive rights under copyright, any use of this publication to "train" generative artificial intelligence (AI) technologies to generate text is expressly prohibited. The author reserves all rights to license uses of this work for generative AI training and development of machine learning language models.

Down & Out Books
3959 Van Dyke Road, Suite 265
Lutz, FL 33558
DownAndOutBooks.com

The characters and events in this book are fictitious. Any similarity to real persons, living or dead, is coincidental and not intended by the author.

Cover design by Chris Orlet

ISBN: 1-64396-416-X
ISBN-13: 978-1-64396-416-4

For Yosh and Joan

> Such things happened in towns of the Middle West, on farms near town, when I was a boy.
> —Sherwood Anderson, *Death in the Woods*

PART I

IRON MOUNTAIN

CHAPTER 1

I STILL DON'T KNOW why he picked me. Or why he picked any of us. If I had to guess—if you put a gun to my head—I'd say it was because we were easy marks. We weren't the popular kids or the cool kids or the dean's listers.

I sure wasn't.

I was one of those unexceptional, day-dreamy kids—the kind of guy who, when you look back thirty-five years later at your high school yearbook, you have no recollection of ever having seen before. There are a great many of us and nobody knows what happened to us after high school. What's more, nobody cares.

Now that I think about it, I should have been the last person he picked. Me or Kevin. Me, because I was his boss's nephew (my uncle was pastor of our church) and Kevin on account of his dad being a police officer. But in some sick, twisted way I'll never understand that must have made picking us even more enticing.

He sure didn't pick us because we were friends. The only one I liked even a little was James, and we were no longer close. We'd gone our separate ways freshman year when he found some cooler nerds to hang with. But that's high school—the graveyard of boyhood friendships. I made a brief, half-hearted attempt to befriend a few of the other nerds in my class, but in the end I decided I was better off alone, sitting by myself at lunch reading a cheap paperback novel—the telltale sign of a total loser.

As for Kevin, he and I had long been mortal enemies. His family was Polish, or one of those East European nationalities, and his dad was a St. Louis County cop. A dirty one, rumor had it. The kind who always kept an extra, untraceable automatic in his cruiser in case he needed to shoot an unarmed Black kid and had to plant a gun quick. Kevin was all muscle and bone and sharp edges, a budding sadist who delighted in bullying boys like me, guys who were tall, but didn't have much meat on their bones. Like a lot of tall, skinny kids, I was a natural-born bully magnet, and since I had few friends there was really no downside to picking on me. Nobody was going to step in and say, "Hey asshole, leave Roy the hell alone." Not even my older brother. *Especially* not my brother, who never lacked for a punching bag as long as I was around.

While I didn't particularly enjoy scrapping with Kevin, I could often give back as good as I got. Fighting back was supposed to make a bully think twice, but I don't think Kevin was capable of thinking even once. We only tussled three times, always on the school playground at recess, and I was able to hold my own each time—which surprised the hell out of everyone, including me. But I was sure glad when the teachers finally stepped in and broke things up before I got killed.

Dennis I knew very little about. He was James's cousin—second cousin, I believe. He was short and wiry and snaggle-toothed with frizzy, sand-colored hair that looked like he'd stuck his finger in a light socket. Everything about Dennis screamed "white trash," from his Hoosier drawl to his thrift store threads. He did have one saving grace, though: he could be funny. Funny in a creepy-ventriloquist-doll sort of way. I could never quite figure Dennis out. One minute he'd be quoting scripture like a budding religious scholar and the next he'd be heaving a brick through a dime store window and making off with a toaster. "What? I had a hankering for toast," he'd say. Dennis briefly attended our Catholic school in the sixth grade and again eighth-grade year. After that he disappeared off my radar screen—until that summer, anyway. The only other thing I knew about Dennis was that he lived alone with his mother, who was some kind of extremely devout religious kook. That and he had an uncle on death row.

Some three years earlier, Dennis's Uncle Greg had murdered a woman named Joanna King and her two-year-old son Douglas. *Butchered* might be the more accurate term. The Kings had the great misfortune of living next door to Greg Hailey. All that summer there were stories about the killings in the *St. Louis Globe-Democrat,* which I delivered to seventy-two households every weekday afternoon. The photos that ran with the stories showed a gaunt, creepy guy with long, shaggy black hair, long fingernails, and dark, empty eyes that were like gazing into the bottomless pit of hell. Those images were not something a twelve-year-old newsboy could easily forget.

According to the newspaper accounts, Joanna King ran an unlicensed childcare business out of her home in Affton, Missouri. And on June 23, 1975, Mrs. Terri Sternau, of nearby Glenview, went to drop off her three-year-old daughter at Miss King's little clapboard disaster of a home. No one answered. Concerned and running late for her teller job at a nearby credit union, Mrs. Sternau drove to a corner gas station and telephoned police. An officer kicked in the door and found Joanna King lying face down on the kitchen floor in a puddle of blood. Little Douglas lay lifeless in his blood-soaked toddler bed. Joanna and Douglas King had been stabbed with a hunting knife a total of eighty-seven times, give or take. For some reason we'll never know, the little boy had been disemboweled.

When the officer rushed out to his cruiser to call in the double homicide, a neighbor man poked his head out a bedroom window. "Hello," said the neighbor. "Was anything taken?" The police officer thought that was an odd thing to say, so he asked the neighbor if he would step outside. When the neighbor strode around the side of his house, the officer noticed that his clothes were covered in what appeared to be copious amounts of blood.

The police officer asked the neighbor why he was covered in blood.

"Oh, that's not mine," the neighbor said.

Uncle Greg was taken in for questioning. After obtaining a search warrant, police found all the evidence they would ever need and then some under a mattress that lay on the floor in the corner of Uncle Greg's tiny bedroom. They found Joanna King's purse and some cheap jewelry and a bottle of her cut-rate wine and a near-empty pack of cigarettes and a bloody hunting knife. Not long after that, Uncle Greg judged he was ready to talk. He was taken to a small interrogation room, where a detective asked Uncle Greg why he killed the lady and her kid.

"I dunno," he said.

"You don't know?"

Uncle Greg shook his head. "No clue."

"But you admit you killed them?"

"I guess so."

"But you don't know why?"

"Yeah. It doesn't make any sense."

The detective cleared his throat. "You didn't hear any voices telling you to do it or anything like that?"

"Voices? Nope. Sorry."

I kept reading the newspaper stories, hoping to learn something about why Greg Hailey killed Joanna and Douglas King, but I don't think the police or anyone else ever found out.

Normally I only read the sports pages, but that summer I read every article about the murder of Joanna and Douglas King I could find. I was obsessed. I was twelve years old. I didn't know people were capable of such things. But after that summer I knew better.

I just didn't know why.

JACKS FORK

***

WHAT HAPPENED WAS that the associate pastor at our church, Father Ted Delaney, called up our parents and said he wanted to take a couple of boys on a camping trip to the Mark Twain National Forest for a couple days, and would their son like to go along? It wasn't pitched as a spiritual opportunity (which would have been a deal-killer for us boys), just a fun adventure trip with a hip, young priest. No need for tents because we'd be staying in a quaint, rustic cabin. Today, an invitation like that would send up about a thousand red flags. Today, no priest in his right mind would even contemplate a trip like that. But this was in the Seventies, and Seventies America was a very weird place.

That night at dinner my parents told me about their conversation with Father Ted and asked me if I had any interest in going canoeing with him and some other boys.

"Which other boys?" I asked suspiciously.

They weren't sure. Just some other boys from our parish.

I hesitated. I didn't like not knowing who was going. What if it were three popular kids who'd spend the whole time either making fun of me or shunning me? (Given the choice, I'd prefer shunning.) Then again, I'd never been on a float trip before. My family had vacationed once in the Mark Twain National Forest and I'd enjoyed splashing around in the cold, clear, spring-fed rivers catching buckets of minnows and crawdads and tadpoles. And I liked Father Ted all right. Unlike my uncle, the pastor, who was in his late fifties and rarely said anything except "Get a haircut"—unlike him, Father Ted drove a candy-apple red Ford Mustang with a kickass stereo, and sometimes after early Mass he'd drive us altar boys to the donut shop where he'd treat us to pastries.

I could tell my parents wanted me to go; it was plastered all over their faces. I guess they were both concerned about my inability to make and keep friends. Even dorky friends like

James.

What the hell. I had nothing else going on. I said I'd go.

WE PLANNED TO meet at the rectory at eleven o'clock Wednesday morning. The other guys were already there when my dad dropped me off, stretched out on the back steps of the school: James Fischer, little Dennis Hailey and that bastard Kevin Przybysz. Not a popular kid in the group. About all we had in common was that none of us were considered cool or particularly smart or good athletes or much of anything.

Kevin, James and Dennis had already stowed their duffels and sleeping bags in the back of the vehicle, an old red Jeep Wagoneer with a strip of side wood paneling and a loose luggage rack on the roof. Evidently we were not taking Father Ted's Mustang.

Kevin glanced up. "I already called shotgun," he said. "And these two dorks called the back seat."

I hadn't been expecting a warm, friendly welcome. At most a "What's up?" But I guess even that was too much to ask. I dropped my ratty sleeping bag and duffel at my feet. "So where's that leave me?"

"Not my problem," Kevin said.

"In the back with the bags," Dennis said.

That was fine with me. I preferred to have my own little space I could stretch out in. That's what I told myself, anyway. I went around to the back of the Jeep and dropped the tailgate and tossed in my bags. There was literally no room left for me, unless I sprawled on top of the bags and the coolers.

"And keep off our bags, Doofus," Kevin said.

Doofus. My old grade-school nickname. It had followed me right into high school. God, I hated it. Especially when someone said it in front of a cute girl, which was naturally their favorite time to say it. One of the popular assholes—Toby Rogers—had come up with it. I swore I'd get even with the lousy son of a bitch someday.

I left the tailgate down—the day was already scorching, nearing ninety degrees—and I joined the others on the shaded back steps of the school. "So whose Jeep is this?" I asked.

James removed his Coke-bottle glasses, breathed on the thick lenses, and wiped them with the hem of his polo shirt. "We think it's the Franklins."

I thought I recognized the old beater. Besides being friends with my parents, the Franklins were this super-active family from our parish, always first to volunteer to serve coffee and donuts after Mass or teach Sunday school or man the dunk tank at the homecoming picnic. Mr. and Mrs. Franklin had themselves a stable full of pretty little daughters—five in total. Not a single boy. Mary Beth Franklin was in my class. She was a cheerleader, but not one of those stuck-up girls who go into cheerleading because they want to be popular or show off. She just really enjoyed cheerleading—like some guys are really into model airplanes or baseball-card collecting. I think she would have been crazy about cheerleading if the only school sport was chess club.

"Block that knight! Block that knight!"

The back door of the rectory banged open and Father Ted Delaney bounced down the back steps. I barely recognized him; he had on a pair of mirrored sunglasses and a black guayabera shirt and white Bermuda shorts with a pair of leather sandals and a natty white Panama hat with a wide black band. I wasn't sure if he looked cool or ridiculous. He sure didn't look like a Catholic priest.

He still sounded like one though. He stood at the bottom of the steps and raised his arms skyward and solemnly intoned: "This is the day the Lord has made, let us rejoice and be glad." Then he peered at us over the rim of his mirrored sunglasses. He must have registered our displeasure, because he quickly added, "Okay, I promise that's the last of the Jesus stuff you'll hear from me."

The four of us glanced dubiously at each other.

"What a gorgeous day," he said and clapped his hands together. "Who's ready for an awesome adventure?"

Silence.

"Boys, boys, let's not be stereotypical moody teenagers. Let's have fun, shall we?"

This was met by more moody teenage silence.

"OK then. Are we all loaded up? Ready to weigh anchor?"

Everyone looked at me. I nodded feebly.

Father Ted grinned and dusted off one more nautical cliché. "Fine then. Time to shove off!"

We got to our feet. I went around to the back of the Jeep and crawled into the cramped cargo compartment. I quickly set about rearranging the bags until I had cleared an area large enough where I could squeeze into a modified fetal position. Kevin eased into the passenger side and Dennis and James got into the back seat. Father Ted slid in behind the wheel and cranked the engine and the old Jeep sputtered and rumbled to life.

"Let there be music," said Father Ted. He slipped a tape into the cassette player and a vaguely familiar tune came on. An old, psychedelic folk song. Father Ted sang along, his churchy voice sounding strangely out of place among the secular Sixties' lyrics.

"I'm just mad about Saffron. Saffron's mad about me…"

"Can we listen to something else?" Dennis cried. "How about the radio?"

Father Ted shook his head and kept right on singing, *"They call me Mell-ow Yell-ow…"*

Dennis rolled his eyes. "Good lord, it's gonna be a long drive," he said.

DENNIS WASN'T WRONG. The drive took three hours and some change, much of it down winding two-lane highways that offered few opportunities to pass the countless convoys of combines and harvesters chugging along at fifteen miles per hour. It was pretty though, the countryside. Once you got outside of suburbia the scenery immediately transformed from strip-mall deathscape to a James Herriot novel. Back in the cargo area, however, the atmosphere was less like a charming, pastoral novel and more like a hypersonic wind tunnel. I couldn't hear a word they were saying up front, what with the windows down and Donovan crooning, so I got out the paperback I'd brought along for company. But no sooner had I started reading than I began to feel queasy and carsick, and the last thing I wanted to do was toss up my breakfast over everyone's luggage. I was trying not to piss the other guys off if I could help it. So I put the book away and lay on my back and stared up at the torn fabric ceiling and killed time the way I so often did—feeling sorry for myself and trying not to throw up. It wasn't easy because riding in the back of that Jeep was like swimming in a juice blender. The rear shocks were all shot to hell and by the time we pulled onto Route 67, my brains were as scrambled as a three-egg omelet. Worse, Father Ted was a chain smoker and all that secondhand smoke settled in a big ugly cloud right above my head and had me hacking and wheezing like a lung patient. An hour or so into the ride I noticed that Dennis was smoking too. I knew Dennis was a smoker, but I never thought he'd have the guts to do it in front of our assistant pastor. Nor could I believe that Father Ted let him do it. But I guess that's what the new generation of cool priests did.

They did nothing.

IRON MOUNTAIN, MISSOURI was our destination—or a few miles outside of Iron Mountain, anyway. The town itself looked like every other small mining town in southern Missouri in the 1970s, a cluster of working-class cottages encircling a doddering business district that was unknowingly living on borrowed time. Every tavern, cafe, bank, barber shop, grocery, hardware store, and exotic Protestant church looked like it had seen better days. Four decades later, that same downtown would get a second life as a pseudo-historic district with cutesy, overpriced antique shops, bed-and-breakfasts, art galleries, a coffee shop, even a microbrewery. But at that time no one would have believed that Iron Mountain would be reborn someday as a bush-league tourist attraction.

It turned out we weren't staying in a quaint, rustic cabin after all. Our so-called cabin was a blue tin-sided, one-bedroom house. What you'd call a fixer-upper today, or more likely a tear-down. Half its windows were boarded up, and the other half should have been. The battered roof was missing most of its shingles and years of cast-off debris choked the underbrush and blackberry brambles surrounding the house, while mounds of torn black trash bags littered the front yard. My heart sank into my sneakers as we pulled into the gravel drive. We sat in the Jeep for a moment gazing in sorrowful disbelief at our "quaint, rustic cabin."

"I think we got the wrong place," Kevin said.

Father Ted squinted over the top of his sunglasses. "No," he said. "This is the address. Ain't that right, Dennis?"

"Don't look at me. I ain't ever been here before." Dennis broke into a shit-eating grin now. "If I had, I wouldn't have come back."

We climbed out of the Jeep and stood around stretching out the kinks and blinking at the crappy little house.

"I thought we were staying in a rustic log cabin?" Kevin said, his voice steeped in outrage and disappointment. "Didn't you tell my folks we'd be in a rustic cabin? This looks more like a lost hobo shack."

"Actually it's more like a ranch house," said Father Ted. "A rustic ranch." He coughed in his hand. "The important thing is we have a roof over our heads. Well, part of a roof." He turned to me and James and smiled encouragingly. "Isn't that right, boys?"

I know, fifteen-year-old boys don't usually care where they sleep, be it on porches, hay wagons, treehouses or dirty basement floors. But I did have my heart set on a rustic log cabin, like the one Robert Redford built in that *Jeremiah Johnson* movie.

Ol' Jeremiah Johnson wouldn't have let his horses stay in a dump like this.

Kevin said, "Whose shack is it?"

"Belongs to my uncle," Dennis said.

An icy void opened in my bowels and James and I shared an open-mouthed look.

"Not the one that...not the one on death row?" I said. "Tell me this ain't his shack?"

"Actually—"

"A *differen*t uncle," said Father Ted.

We scrutinized his face trying to determine if he was telling the truth, but with the mirrored sunglasses it was hard to tell. If the eyes are the window to the soul, Father Ted's soul was boarded up, same as the shack. Theoretically, priests weren't supposed to lie; then again Father Ted wasn't your typical priest. Typical priests didn't take fifteen-year-old boys on adventure trips and allow them to smoke cigarettes. If a typical priest caught you smoking cigarettes he'd probably make you smoke the whole pack at one time until you either had an honest-to-God, come-to-Jesus moment or you keeled over dead.

James turned and started back toward the Jeep. "Yeah, I'm not staying in there."

"Me neither," I said.

Father Ted heaved a heavy sigh. "Oh, for crying out loud," he said. "What's it matter whose house it is as long as it's got a roof on it? Well, part of a roof, anyway." He removed his Panama hat and fanned himself with it. "I thought this would be more comfortable than dragging musty tents around and sleeping on the cold ground. And it's got running water and a toilet...or so I was told."

Dennis strode up to one of the windows. He stood on his tiptoes and cupped his hands around his eyes. "I don't see any dismembered bodies inside," he said. "Not yet, anyway."

For the life of me, I couldn't understand why Father Ted had invited Dennis along. He didn't even belong to our parish. Not anymore. Was it because he had access to a free rundown ranch house? Would no one else go? Was he hoping to somehow save Dennis's soul so he wouldn't end up like his Uncle Greg?

"Fine," said Father Ted. "Anyone who doesn't want to stay inside can sleep in the back of the Jeep. Or out in the yard. Deal?"

We shuffled our feet indecisively. I tried to imagine sleeping outdoors in what was essentially a mini-garbage dump or in the Jeep with my bare feet sticking out the back. What if some big old black bear came wandering out of the woods at two in the morning and saw my bare feet sticking out of the Jeep and shuffled over and started licking my toes like in that *Three Stooges* short.

That's the kind of thing you worry about when you waste much of your childhood watching *Three Stooges* shorts.

"Does the back seat fold down?" I asked.

"Couldn't tell you," said Father Ted. He pulled on the screen door and managed to get it open after three hard yanks. The front door, however, was locked with a deadbolt. Father Ted drew a heavy ring of keys from his pocket and tried them one by one on the deadbolt. None of the first five keys worked. I started to get my hopes up. Maybe this *was* the wrong house. Or maybe we didn't have the right key. After the sixth key, Father Ted opened up a string of mumbled curses. It was the first time I'd heard a priest swear like that, but I supposed that's what young, modern priests did. Cursed and smoked and drove sports cars and listened to Sixties rock and hung out with teenage boys.

The seventh key did the trick. We tramped glumly inside and

dumped our bags on the cracked linoleum floor. The inside was steamy and musty and the smell, a bouquet of dead cat, dirty jockstraps and skunk piss, instantly knocked us for a loop. We made a beeline for the windows, but the ones that weren't boarded up were sealed shut by years of dirt and humidity and the occasional flathead nail. Father Ted alone succeeded in forcing a window open. "Praise be!" he cried.

The rest of the windows wouldn't budge, not even for Kevin.

Someone flipped on a light switch. Nothing happened. "Huh," said Father Ted. "I hope the power's not out."

Dennis peered over the top of a torn lamp shade. "Some thieving hillbilly stole the bulbs," he said with a sort of half chuckle. "Probably stole everything that wasn't nailed down." He shook his head and glanced at Father Ted. "My uncle ain't gonna like this."

"Which uncle?" James said.

"Never mind!" cried Father Ted, then he set to work raising the battered aluminum blinds, stirring clouds of long dormant dust particles. "If it weren't for Venetian blinds, it would be curtains for us all," he said with a chuckle.

Nobody laughed.

After the dust settled, we took stock of the room's furnishings: a brown, ratty-looking couch (missing one of the cushions) and a pair of shabby folding chairs that not even Iron County's most hard-up criminal would steal. Beside the couch leaned a three-legged end table on which sat the lamp with the missing bulb. In a far corner of the room stood a tiled kitchenette. A sink and small counter, anyway. From the grease stains on the tile floor you could plainly see where the stove and refrigerator had been before they were looted. Other than that, there was a small 1940s diner table and a couple ragged chairs that looked like they'd collapse the moment you sat on them. Everything in the place looked like it had been bought secondhand from a landfill.

I went to check out the back room: a small bedroom with no

furniture—not even a bedbug infested, blood- and pee-stained mattress on the floor, like you would expect. No TV set, of course. I did find an old dust-covered Motorola radio, but when I plugged it in and turned it on I got nothing—not even static.

James said, "So, where are we supposed to sleep?"

"What's wrong with the floor?" said Father Ted, indicating the dirty linoleum beneath our feet.

Kevin said, "What isn't wrong with it?"

"This place gives me the willies," James said.

Father Ted gave us a look that was both aggrieved and forlorn, and his shoulders slumped perceptibly. He was clearly disappointed in the condition of our lodgings, though he tried to put on a brave face. For a moment I almost felt bad for him.

Almost.

"All we're gonna do is sleep here a couple nights," he said. "The rest of the time we'll be outdoors communing with nature in all her God-given glory. You can rough it for a couple of nights, can't you?" He gazed briefly at the cracked linoleum and the brown water-stained walls. "It beats a musty old tent."

"I'd prefer a musty tent," Dennis said. He plopped down on the couch and was soon engulfed in a cloud of dust. He reminded me of Charlie Brown's friend Pigpen.

Father Ted drew a cigarette from a pack in his shirt pocket. "Well, we didn't bring one so there's no point discussing it." Father Ted lit up a smoke and stepped into the tiny bathroom. A moment later he came out grinning like a sixteen-year-old girl on prom night. "Good news, we have a functioning bathroom!" he announced grandly. "I mean, the toilet works. That's the main thing. There's no light or hot water, but you can't have everything. Besides, we're supposed to be roughing it."

"Yeah, you keep saying that," Kevin said.

Father Ted ignored this. "Anybody hungry? What do you say we bring in the rest of our provisions?"

The four of us boys exchanged a look.

"James? Roy?"

"Sure," I said. It was almost four o'clock and I was half starved and desperate to get back out in the fresh air. I went out to the Jeep and crawled into the cargo compartment and dragged out one of the Igloo coolers. I opened the cooler and peered inside. There were two buckets of cold Kentucky Fried Chicken and biscuits and a container of store-bought potato salad on ice. Kevin and James joined me outside and got the other cooler and the bags of corn chips and three of those forty-ounce glass bottles of Coca-Cola and some paper plates and plastic forks and Styrofoam cups, and we carried it all inside in one trip. We piled everything on the kitchen table and we set about loading our plates with great heaps of cold chicken, biscuits and potato salad. Father Ted said grace (so much for his promise to can the Jesus stuff) and we crowded around the table and chowed down like a clan of ravenous Neanderthals. Nobody felt much like talking.

After we'd eaten, James and I collected the plates and cups and chicken bones and carried everything outside. Since the whole yard was a garbage dump it didn't matter where we tossed the stuff, but good old anal-retentive James managed to find an old tin trash can lying along the side of the house, so we tossed the scraps inside, nice and tidy. Then things got uncomfortably silent. I suddenly felt awkward and stupid. It had been more than a year since we'd last hung out together, since James began snubbing me in earnest. I suppose we were each waiting for the other to say something and neither of us knew what that might be. Would James apologize for being a jerk and unfriending me? I hoped not. That would be even more awkward than saying nothing. Not that I had to worry about it. Apologizing probably never crossed his mind.

Finally James said, "I heard Father Ted took Scott Carroll and Bob Harriman and Toby Rogers snow-skiing."

Scott and Bob and Toby were hands-down the three coolest guys in our class.

"Bet they weren't roughing it in a death row inmate's murder

shack," I said.
"Probably had a chalet with a hot tub."
I nodded.
James turned and headed back inside.
Later, I found out he was mostly right. It had been a luxury A-frame and it did have a hot tub.

BACK INSIDE, DENNIS was trying to get up a game of blackjack. The problem was that no one—with the exception of Father Ted—had anything to wager with. The rest of us were still too young to have real teenager jobs—like fast-food burrito-maker or car washer. We were still at the grass-cutting and paperboy stage of our careers. Dennis said poker wasn't any fun unless you played for some kind of stakes, even if it was just for smokes. And only Dennis and Father Ted had smokes.

"We could always play strip poker," said Father Ted.

There was a long, awkward silence, followed by a few uneasy laughs. Not from me, but from James and Kevin.

"That was a joke," Father Ted put in.

The four of us glanced nervously at each other and James chuckled again, though it sounded more like a death rattle than laughter.

Anyway, card games bored me to tears so I went over and slumped on the couch and tried to read my book. It took a while, but they finally resolved the stakes issue by coming up with an ingenious solution called "Bloody Knuckles." Whoever won the hand got to smack the losers' knuckles with the deck of cards. Judging from the cries of intense pain, it must have hurt like hell. Bloody Knuckles was Dennis's idea, of course, but for some reason Father Ted and the others went along with it. As long as they kept their clothes on I didn't care what they did.

When night drew down and it got too dark to see the cards, Father Ted got to his feet and rubbed his sore knuckles and said we should hit the hay if we wanted to be on the river by seven.

"That means getting up no later than six," he said.

Six! I thought. *Why six?* I was not a morning person. Especially if it wasn't a school day. Wasn't this trip supposed to be about rest and relaxation? Why'd we have to be on the river by seven? Or even nine? What was the goddamn hurry? The river wasn't going anywhere. Only nobody else objected, so I guess I was the only one who felt that way.

Father Ted went over and patted one of the two remaining couch cushions, sending up a mini-dust storm that quickly spread out over the room. "I'll bed down here," he said. Then he drew his toiletry bag from his duffle and padded into the bathroom. We soon heard the cold shower running. The rest of us unrolled our sleeping bags and tried to find a smooth, relatively dead-roach-free zone on the linoleum to stretch out. Like groggy, punch-drunk prize-fighters, we each retreated to a corner of the main room.

No sooner were we bedded down than Kevin began peppering Dennis with questions about his death-row uncle. Was this *really* his house? How many people had he really killed? How were they going to execute him? Gas chamber? Electric chair? Firing squad? Dennis yawned and said he wasn't sure whose house it was—his death-row uncle's or his rapist uncle's or maybe it belonged to his plain, ordinary-crazy homeless uncle. "Well, probably not my homeless uncle, because then he wouldn't be homeless, now would he?"

I couldn't tell if he was joking or what. Dennis's mind was so twisted you could never get a straight answer out of him. Kevin wouldn't drop the subject. What was Uncle Greg really like? Had Dennis ever seen him do anything really crazy? What kind of car did he drive and what kind of music did he listen to? It seemed like a bad idea to me, dwelling on his uncle and his bloody crimes, but strangely Dennis didn't seem to mind. Nor did he have anything really gory to share. He did, however, tell us that shortly after his uncle was sentenced to death, his unhinged holy-roller mother hired an exorcist to make sure their house was free of evil spirits (even though Uncle Greg had only been a guest in the home a handful of times). The local bishop didn't want any part of it, so Mrs. Hailey had to find a priest from a more conservative breakaway sect of the Catholic church to perform the ritual, which he was happy to do for a price. Dennis had been present for the exorcism and he said it had freaked the shit out of him.

"Scariest thing I ever seen. Doors slamming on their own. Creepy voices coming out of nowhere. The priest getting the shit kicked out of him by dark, unseen forces."

"Yeah, we've all seen *The Exorcist*," Kevin said. "Couldn't you at least come up with one original detail that wasn't in the movie?"

"What movie is that?" said Father Ted. He stood in the bathroom doorway toweling off. I looked away so I didn't have to glimpse his big, white, flabby ass.

"*The Exorcist*," Kevin said.

"A blasphemous film," said Father Ted. "The Catholic bishops have condemned it. You are forbidden from seeing it."

"I've already seen it twice," Kevin said.

"Three times," said James.

Father Ted was the first to doze off that night and he snored like Fred Fucking Flintstone. The rest of us stayed up past midnight, talking quietly, trying to freak each other out with scary stories. ("How many women do you think Uncle Greg buried beneath these floorboards?") Around one a.m. the others drifted off to sleep—all except me and Dennis. He had gotten hold of James's flashlight and an ashtray and he was smoking cigarettes and reading an Andy Capp paperback and chuckling crazily to himself.

Around two a.m. I asked Dennis if he minded putting out his cigarette. "I'd rather not die tonight in a fire in a shack in Bumblefuck, Missourah," I said.

Dennis raised up on his elbow and shined the flashlight in my eyes.

"Don't worry, Doofus," he said. "Nobody's gonna die. Not tonight anyway." Then he laughed his kooky laugh and stubbed out his cigarette on the linoleum floor.

I probably got two hours sleep that night.

No, not even that much.

CHAPTER 2

MORNING BROKE CLOUDY and cool. I stood on the front steps of the shack gazing over the trash-strewn front yard at a lush green Ozark valley echoing with birdsong and, farther away, the buzz of a chainsaw. A thick gray fog floated lazily through the distant St. Francois Mountains. The French have a word for this kind of glaring juxtaposition. They call it *jolie laide*. But us Midwesterners can't seem to grasp the concept of something being beautiful and ugly at the same time, even though that's probably the natural state of things. Anyway, that's what I was thinking about when Father Ted slipped up behind me holding a mug of instant coffee and puffing on the day's first cigarette.

"And some poor misguided fools think this was all random, that it all happened by chance," he said.

"You mean the chainsaw?" I said.

"Let's load up the Jeep, OK?" said Father Ted.

I choked down a stale Danish and a cup of orange juice and waited for the others to join us outside, then we piled into the Jeep for the twenty-mile drive to Harvey's Canoe Rental and Sales.

Harvey's was a local landmark, an old sheet-metal garage covered in peeling blue and tan paint. The store had your requisite pair of rusted ice freezers on its sagging front porch and the obligatory tick-infested, three-legged mutt out front barking its fool head off. If you didn't know better you'd think Harvey's was one of those cultural clichés, like those double-decker outhouses they have at Silver Dollar City. Like the owner had to special-order the three-legged mutt and rusted freezers. ("Sorry Harv, all we got in stock are four-legged dogs and new, pristine ice merchandizers.")

We goofed off in the parking lot (well, mostly Dennis goofed off) while Father Ted went in and paid for the canoes, then we climbed into a muddy Chevy van with a pair of battle-scarred canoes lashed to its roof. One of Harvey's kids drove, a scrawny, loquacious little fella with hair in his eyes and a Camel filter crammed in his mouth. He could have been Dennis's country twin. He didn't look old enough to drive, but he took us upriver anyway, some twenty-five miles, and dropped us off at a remote access point. His name was D.J. and he had the thickest, mushiest country accent I'd ever heard. He may as well have been speaking Swahili. I think he said we'd be floating back down to Harvey's and that the whole trip would take between four and six hours, depending on how many times we stopped or fell out of our canoes. But that's only a guess. He said we were lucky because the river was up on account of all the storms they'd been having. I didn't feel lucky. I'd gotten less than two hours sleep thanks to Dennis hopping up every twenty minutes and rooting through his bags (looking for what, I wondered...an Andy Capp comic? Cigarettes? A machete?) or staring out the window into the pitch-black night, or just generally being a creepy-ass weirdo. As long as he was skulking around I was afraid to close my eyes.

D.J. got our canoes in the water and when we turned around to thank him, he and the van were already gone. Nothing but a trail of dust and the fading sound of a knocking, hissing engine and the rush of the river.

There was only one way out now.

We paired up and, just as I feared, I got teamed up with

Kevin. I wanted to protest, but I wasn't sure how to do that without making him angry. I saw no point in pissing him off before we even got on the river. Not that it mattered. From the moment we pushed off he was badgering the hell out of me.

"You're doing it all wrong, Doofus!"

"Paddle on the other side!"

"Who taught you how to paddle? Flunky the Clown?"

"Faster! Harder!"

Dennis, James and Father Ted climbed into the other canoe. I could hear them somewhere behind us, laughing and singing and having a gay old time. Meanwhile dark clouds of buffalo gnats and deerflies big as bats swarmed our canoe (or at least my end of the canoe). The vicious little bastards were relentless, though I much preferred them to my canoe partner. I swore if Kevin snapped at me one more time I was going to bash him over the head with the business end of my oar. Though when the time came to clobber him, I couldn't do it. I lacked the killer instinct. So I gritted my teeth and paddled on.

D.J. was right about the river. The water was high and the current was strong and there were long spells of flat water where—theoretically at least—we could have floated peacefully and used both hands to slap mosquitoes and black flies. But Kevin wouldn't hear of that. I'd made the rookie mistake of getting in the front of the canoe where he could supervise every move I made, and if I stopped paddling for more than a few seconds he would start in on me, like I was costing us the America's Cup.

Jacks Fork sounds like a small-town cafe, but in fact it's one of the Current River's larger and wilder tributaries, and the Fork was certainly the place to be that morning, judging by the number of people on the river. A mix of local hillbillies and their dogs and college kids, all of them determined to drink as much beer and make as much racket as possible. And all of them having a hell of a time. Father Ted and Dennis and James and even Kevin seemed to be enjoying themselves, too. I was the only sourpuss. The only killjoy. What was wrong with me? Why couldn't I have a good time like other people? Why was I constitutionally incapable of enjoying myself? Why did everyone else's idea of fun strike me as ignorant, boorish behavior?

I wasn't sure then, and I'm not sure now.

About that time we came upon the first set of rapids. "Rapids" is a bit of an exaggeration. "Riffles" might be the more accurate term. But even so, Father Ted's canoe managed to turn over in one choppy patch of water and all three of them took an unexpected swim. Nobody got hurt, but we lost all of our supplies. Later we found our cooler a quarter mile downriver, but our lunch and drinks were long gone.

I don't want to give the impression that riding the river was all bad. The water was cold and clear and high, so we didn't have to get out and carry the canoes very often. And the weather was good, at least in the morning. (By afternoon, it was a scorcher.) And the scenery was pretty—for the Midwest, anyway—with the oaks and pines and limestone bluffs, and the chittering birds and the burbling streams. When there weren't other people around to spoil it. And this was the Seventies, so there wasn't all the plastic trash and litter and the loud ATVs you find on the river nowadays. Still, I would have preferred to simply wade around in the water rather than paddle my ass off like a galley slave, which is what it felt like.

I don't know how long we were on the river that day. Six hours. Eight hours. Long enough to get the hell bitten out of me and the top layer of my skin burned off. Long enough for me to contemplate killing Kevin a half dozen times. I was never so grateful as when we rounded that last bend in the river and the Harvey's Canoe Rental and Sales sign came into view above the treeline. As soon as I saw the sign I jumped out of the canoe and swam for shore, ignoring Kevin's curses and harangues.

Later, as we made our way up the hillpath to Harvey's, Kevin couldn't resist one last chance to mess with me. "Well, that was fun," he said. "I can't wait to do it again tomorrow." And here he gave me a sharp sock on the arm. "And tomorrow you better have your shit together, Doofus."

CHAPTER 3

IT WAS A RELIEF to be on dry land again—dry land being the dirt and gravel lot of Harvey's Canoe Rental and Sales. We slouched sunburned and exhausted on the Jeep's tailgate, while Father Ted went to get our deposit back. Four unsupervised teenage boys alone on a hot summer afternoon. What could possibly go wrong?

Right on cue, Dennis slipped a small jackknife from his back pocket and expertly snapped it open. The sun glinted off the blade. This was no dull Boy Scout knife; it was the real deal. "Any of you pussies wanna play chicken?"

James and I shared a look of existential dread.

"The object is to see how close to your foot I can stick the blade without you jumping out of the way," Dennis said.

"I know how to play chicken," Kevin said.

What the hell was taking Father Ted so long? I thought.

"Cool, I'll go first." Dennis squinted up one eye and took aim at my shoeless left foot. I drew back a few steps. Dennis crept a few steps forward, still concentrating on my bare foot. "You move, you're *Bok! Bok! Bok!*"

I didn't want to be chicken, but I didn't want to have one of my toes pointlessly amputated either.

"Knock it off, Dennis," James told his cousin. "We're probably three hours from the nearest hospital."

"Buncha pussies," Dennis said and before I could react he flung the knife at my foot. The knife landed blade-first in the gravel. It missed taking off my little toe by an eighth of an inch.

"Whoa!" Dennis said. "Beat that, fuckers!"

A wash of adrenaline crashed over me, bringing with it a sick, dizzying feeling way down in the pit of my stomach. *That's it,* I thought. I pulled the knife out of the gravel and turned and hurled it as far as I could across the highway into a stand of pines. Then I braced myself for battle. I had height and weight on Dennis, but he had the advantage when it came to sheer batshit craziness. He hopped around in front of me like a small vanilla Joe Frazier sundae with extra nuts.

"That was my best knife!" he cried, throwing air punches at my face. "Now go get it, fuckhead!"

I glared back at him, determined not to back down. "Get it yourself, you freaking lunatic."

James and Kevin moved back, giving us plenty of room to kill each other. Dennis and I circled each other like two wary alley cats sizing each other up. He made a couple of elaborate fakes, but held his punches, no doubt waiting for me to drop my guard.

I felt ridiculous fighting Dennis. I was a good foot taller, maybe more. At the same time I was scared shitless that he would pull another knife out of his back pocket.

"Who's hungry?"

Father Ted stood behind Kevin and James. He stuffed a wad of bills into his front pocket and said, "I thought we'd stop at that little café we passed on the way here. I do love a small-town café. They're either really great or really horrible." He grinned and shook his head. "It's always a crapshoot."

Dennis was still crouched in an offensive stance, coiled and ready to strike.

Father Ted glanced at us, a quizzical look on his face. "What's going on?"

I let my hands drop, then I shoved past Kevin and James and

strode hurriedly to the Jeep—shaken, but relieved to be in one piece. I crawled across the open tailgate into the cargo compartment and pulled up the gate behind me. When I looked back, I saw Dennis tramping across the road toward the woods.

"Dennis?" Father Ted called. His gaze shifted to Kevin and James. "Where's he going?"

James shrugged. "Nature calls, I guess."

Father Ted snorted loudly. "Can't ignore nature," he said. "Not out here, anyways."

ON THE WAY to the café I drew out my wallet and counted the bills inside. I had a grand total of six dollars and that had to last me the rest of the trip. (How much would a bowl of tomato soup and a glass of ice water set me back?) It's a lousy feeling, being the only one without money. Usually it wasn't a problem for me; we lived in a poor working-class neighborhood so none of my friends or neighbors had any money either. But James and Kevin and Dennis weren't from my neighborhood.

By rights I should have been flush with cash. I was a paperboy with an eight-block route. Only my route was a complete bust. The route was in the same poor working-class neighborhood we lived in and the folks I delivered the paper to were mostly deadbeats, which was ironic because if I was a minute late with the paper they would be on the phone to our house asking my mother where the hell their paper was, like the newspaper was an ambulance taking them to the emergency room or something. When I'd finally arrive at their house with my sack of papers they'd be waiting impatiently at the screen door.

"About time you got here. Why're you so late?"

I wanted to say, "Why are you such a deadbeat?" But I never did. I was never big on confrontations.

Or maybe I was just a coward.

Of course, when Friday afternoon rolled around and it was

time to collect the subscription money, the deadbeats were nowhere to be found. I'd pound on their doors and peek in their windows, certain they were hiding inside somewhere, just waiting for me to leave the paper and go away—which is what I did. I slunk away without the subscription money. This was a big deal because every week I had to pay back the newspaper office. The deal was I would pay off the circulation manager, and he would give me something back. I don't know how much I was supposed to get back because I never got anything back. I always owed the circulation manager money because of all the deadbeats on my route.

The newspaper route had been my dad's idea. He thought it would teach me a valuable lesson about Free Market Capitalism and the Protestant Work Ethic, even though we were Catholic and the Protestants were all going to hell.

The crazy part was my dad would have to make up the difference. And this was never easy because my dad was flat broke most of the time. It's hard to get rich as an aluminum-siding salesman when you're always hungover and you don't crawl out of bed until noon. Still, his faith in Capitalism and the Protestant Work Ethic never wavered—no matter how much money we lost.

In a way I suppose I did learn a valuable lesson about Capitalism. I learned that if you work your ass off, if you trudge through knee-high snow all winter, and tramp through 100-degree afternoons all summer lugging a heavy newspaper bag you'll end up owing money to The Man. And when it's time to eat at some crappy little diner in some southern Missouri ghost town you'll be all freaked out because you only got six bucks to last three days.

So it came as a relief when Father Ted said that lunch was on him. Thank God diocesan priests don't take a vow of poverty like other religious orders do. I guess that's why he could afford that sweet new Ford Mustang.

The little café was called The Iron Skillet. (Iron Mountain

wasn't large enough for chain fast-food restaurants like a Dairy Queen and judging from the numerous empty storefronts it never would be.) During lunch I sat across from Dennis, who had us all cracking up with his weird-ass antics, which included the old gag of sucking down half a bottle of tabasco sauce (the trick, he said, was to pour it straight down your gullet, bypassing the lips, taste buds and tongue). We watched fascinatedly as Dennis's face grew fire-engine red and he leapt to his feet and bolted out the front door of the diner like a beheaded chicken.

I had been worried that Dennis would be pissed at me for throwing his stupid knife into the woods, but if he was he didn't show it. He only kicked me under the table twice and he wasn't wearing steel-toed boots, so it didn't hurt too much. And after he swallowed the bottle of tabasco sauce he seemed to lose interest in me.

After stuffing ourselves with southern-fried chicken, mashed potatoes and white gravy, mac and cheese and sweet tea (except for Dennis, whose lunch consisted of a half-gallon of milk and six glasses of ice water), we drove back to the ranch. We were all bug-bit and sunburned and dead tired and I for one just wanted to crawl up in a corner and fall asleep. The house, however, was dark and stuffy and still smelled like raccoon piss. In other words, it was still unfit for human habitation—even for fifteen-year-old boys, so we propped open the front and back doors and went back outside and loafed around the yard until the rooms aired out and the night air cooled off. We scoured the property until we found something to sit on: a busted wooden side chair, a rusted wash tub, a pair of cracked red milk crates.

Then Father Ted asked, "Who's up for a card game later?"

I remembered his crack about strip poker and kept my mouth shut.

"I'm in," Kevin said.

James shrugged his shoulders. "Sure. Nothing else to do."

Dennis, who seemed to have mostly recovered from his tabasco debacle, scratched the back of his neck and said, "Only if it's high-stakes poker."

Kevin said, "What's a punk like you know about high stakes?"

"Goddamnit," Father Ted said, knitting his brow in consternation. "We forgot to get light bulbs."

"Ohhh, somebody took the Lord's name in vain," Dennis said. "Somebody's gonna have to go to confession."

Father Ted bit back a grin. "Boys, the sacrament of reconciliation is an opportunity to recover the grace of God's friendship and as such it should not be taken lightly."

"Yeah, well if my mother heard you say that she'd wash your mouth out with lye soap," Dennis said.

"I'm sure she would." Father Ted stared off, thinking. "I guess I'll run back into town and get some bulbs so we aren't bumping into the walls all night." Then he hesitated. "And something to drink." Father Ted's steady gaze fell on me as he spoke. "What kind of beer would you like?"

I wasn't sure who he was talking to. I glanced around at the others; they were all staring at me with wide eyes that seemed to exclaim: *He's talking to you, Doofus! Do not screw this up!*

"Um," I said. The question had caught me off guard. It wasn't a question I ever expected to hear from a priest. Or from anybody. Like a beautiful senior girl walking up to me and saying, *Do you want a blowjob now or after school?*

I froze up.

I knew the guys were counting on me not to screw this up. And if I did screw it up, they'd never let me forget it. And that made the pressure more intense.

"Well?" said Father Ted.

What kind of beer? The only kinds of beer I knew were Budweiser, Busch and Stag, and I hadn't liked any of them. They all tasted like sewer water, or how I might imagine sewer water would taste, never having actually drank any. Kids my age were always talking about how you get used to the terrible taste of beer, but I could never understand why you would want to get used to something terrible if you didn't have to. Like getting used to being kicked in the balls. I got the getting-drunk part; what I didn't get was why adult beverages had to taste like someone pissed in a bottle of turpentine.

Dennis ambled up beside me, hands crammed into his back pockets. He not so subtly elbowed me in the side and hissed in my ear: "Tell him what kind of beer you want, Doofus."

The pressure was on. I tried to think of a kind of beer my father *didn't* drink. Maybe it would taste better than the crap he *did* drink. And just like that a name popped into my head. "Pabst," I said.

"Excellent choice," said Father Ted.

Father Ted sure knew how to make a fifteen-year-old boy feel important. Compliment him on his choice of shitty beer. Then he took the other guys' orders—they all wanted Anheuser-Busch products. I thought about changing to Busch—maybe they knew something about Pabst I didn't—but I was hesitant to. I didn't want to give Father Ted a reason to reconsider the whole deal.

Hmmm, can't make up your mind, eh? Maybe you're not mature enough for a beer after all.

Father Ted turned around and asked Dennis, "How's about coming to town with me? Help carry the stuff?"

Dennis studied his sneakers for a long time, like he was looking to them for direction. His sneakers must have said, "Go on, give him a hand," because he soon shrugged his shoulders and mumbled, "Sure."

They eased into the Jeep and Father Ted gave the horn a brief tap and the rest of us a wave. Dennis sat looking glum, like he was auditioning for the role of funeral director in the spring play. They pulled onto the county highway headed toward town, then we lost sight of them.

The three of us shared a look. I half expected James and Kevin to start high-fiving each other, yelling *Whoa dude! We're gonna get shitfaced tonight!* But nobody said anything. Apparently we were going to play it cool. Like what just happened was no big deal. Business as usual. Certainly nobody said anything about how weird it was that a priest was buying a bunch of fifteen-year-old boys a shitload of beer.

Or maybe it wasn't weird. Maybe this was what happened when you turned fifteen…some kind of strange religious rite of passage, like a Bar Mitzvah or a vision quest. I was fifteen and there were still a lot of things I didn't know. But a shitload of beer? I kind of doubted it.

"How about a couple hands of seven-card stud?" Kevin said.

"Okay," James said.

"No thanks," I said.

"Nobody asked you," Kevin said.

I ignored him and went inside to get my book. It was going to be hard to concentrate on the story with a six-pack of cold beer on its way, but I had to do something to kill the time. And I'd rather kill it reading a good book than playing cards with those two dipshits. The book I'd brought along was one of my sister's cheap paperbacks. She didn't mind if I borrowed her books as long as I didn't lose them and I returned them in relatively good condition. They were the only books in our house and they were her personal property. She had about forty well-thumbed paperbacks on a small antique bookshelf beside her bed. I didn't know it at the time but the books were all classics. There was your Hemingway, your Fitzgerald, your Steinbeck, your Brontë sisters. There was Thomas Wolfe and Sylvia Plath and John Cheever and Joseph Heller and Carson McCullers and James Baldwin and even some Doonesbury cartoon books. My sister had an old air conditioner, too—one of those small but heavy window units. It was the only air conditioner on the upstairs floor. She had bought it with her earnings from working the counter at the neighborhood Burger Chef. When my sister was at work—and when I wasn't busy giving away free newspapers to deadbeats—I would sneak into her room and lay on the floor (I would never lay on her bed;

that would have been going too far) and luxuriate in the frosty air conditioning. Sometimes I would listen to her record collection, which was very early Seventies eclectic (The Carpenters, Linda Ronstadt, Bread, The Nitty Gritty Dirt Band, Carole King, Jackson Browne, James Taylor and Willie Nelson). If I was really bored I might glance through the paperbacks on her bookshelf. I was probably the perfect age for some of those writers—guys like Hemingway and Fitzgerald and Thomas Wolfe. Now that I'm older they don't interest me so much, but back then I believed that great books held some kind of magic key, some kind of transformational secrets that would turn me from the lame kid I was into...well I wasn't sure what. Something better, anyway. That's all it took. Reading Hemingway and Steinbeck and Irwin Shaw.

Boy, was I wrong. Not that I blame Steinbeck and Shaw. They didn't have a whole lot to work with.

The book I'd smuggled out of my sister's bedroom was called *Bound for Glory*. It was the autobiography of Woody Guthrie, a Depression-era folk singer/hobo/communist known mostly for writing "This Land Is Your Land." And while I was pretty much indifferent to that classic American folk song, his true-life story was a real page-turner.

I wondered how my sister had come upon a book like *Bound for Glory*. Had she picked it up randomly in a used bookstore and skimmed the back cover and thought, *"A communist hobo folk singer, this sounds interesting?"* In those pre-Internet days an introspective teenager might spend hours in a used book or record store just browsing the collections. If you were lucky you'd find a book like *Bound for Glory* or a record like *Music from Big Pink* and suddenly strange new doors would open up, leading you down twisty, unfamiliar paths and suddenly your whole life would have changed in small and unexpected ways, and, the next thing you knew you were a divorced mailman who hosted open mics at the local coffeehouse on Thursday evenings.

Anyway...

I carried my book outside to read in the fading daylight. In a few minutes the big orange sun would begin to sink below the ridgeline, but for now the warm, bright evening lingered. I sat down on a crack milk crate and found my place in the book and before long I was transported to a wild oil boomtown in north Texas, circa 1918.

It sure seemed preferable to a dead mining town in southern Missouri, circa 1978.

CHAPTER 4

A CYCLONE WAS tearing through Okemah, Oklahoma, a little oil boomtown smack in the middle of Tornado Alley, right around the time of the First World War, when James strode outside and drew up a milk crate and sat down beside me. He *would* have to wait for the most exciting part of the story to show up. I tried to ignore him, keeping my nose buried in the book and hoping he'd get the message. No such luck. Finally, I gave it up and set the book in my lap. "What happened to your card game?" I said.

"We're gonna wait until the others get back. It's no fun with just two people."

I didn't think it was fun with four people either.

The wind had picked up, stirring the branches and rustling the leaves high in the oaks and the hickories and the maples, and bending the more willowy trees nearly sidewise. The kind of gusts you get before a serious cold front blows in. That would have been fine by me. Maybe the rest of the trip would get rained out and we could go home early.

James stared across the front yard, shoulders slumped. Then he turned and gazed at me thoughtfully like he was trying to decide whether to tell me some deep, dark secret. A moment passed, then he finally came out with it. "You know it wasn't my idea to bring Dennis."

I shrugged. "I never said it was."

"Yeah, well in case you were thinking it."

Since when does he care what I think? I thought.

"Dennis and Father Ted used to be close," he said. "You know Dennis's mom."

"Yeah, she's cuckoo for Cocoa Puffs."

"Yeah, well, she wanted Dennis to be a priest, so they used to hang out a lot."

"Dennis, a priest?"

"Yeah well, she had to give up on that idea. Now she'd be happy if he just stayed out of juvenile detention."

I nodded, wondering what any of this had to do with me. I watched a couple of miniature dust devils form by the county road, whirl and spin themselves out. Apparently James was going to be my friend for a day or two, then go back to shunning me. No thanks. Just leave me alone and let me get back to my book, which was a hell of a lot more interesting than he was.

James nodded toward the book in my hand. "Whatcha reading? Something gay?"

"I don't know. Are cyclones gay?"

"The ones in books are."

"This one seems pretty non-gay to me. Destroyed a bunch of houses."

"Cool."

I dog-eared the page and closed the book. The World War I Oklahoma cyclone would have to wait.

James reached for the book. "Can I see it?"

I hesitated. "What for?"

"I just want to see it."

"It isn't mine."

"Whose is it?"

I didn't want to tell him it belonged to my sister; he'd give me some shit about reading a girl's book and I wasn't in the mood for that. I tossed him the book. He flipped through the pages, pausing at Woody Guthrie's scribbly drawings. He seemed underwhelmed by the whole thing.

"What is this? Hoboes? You're reading a book about hoboes?"

"No…Yeah. What's wrong with hoboes? Hoboes are cool."

"Yeah, hoboes, bums, freeloaders—all very cool."

I stewed silently. Goddamnit, Woody Guthrie *was* cool. And James was a dork. And I was glad we were no longer friends.

I said, "What's that idiot Kevin doing?"

He tossed the book back to me. "Don't know, don't care." Then his eyes narrowed as he studied me. "Did you know who was going on this trip?"

"No. Did you?"

"If you'd known would you have gone?"

"Not a chance."

James stared off, thinking. "Kevin and Dennis don't bother me. I can get along with anybody."

This was his subtle way of saying that I couldn't. Anyway, it wasn't true that he could get along with anyone. At school, the cool kids laughed at him behind his back. Sometimes right in his face.

James got still and didn't move. Maybe there was something else he wanted to get off his chest. Maybe he wanted to apologize for unfriending me. Or at least tell me why he did it.

I was kidding myself. Guys never say those kinds of things to each other. Girls might…I wouldn't know. But guys, never.

"Tomorrow I'm going in Father Ted's canoe," I said.

"Kevin says you're riding with him."

"I don't care what that butthole says."

James shrugged. "Dennis ain't much better. He tipped us on purpose."

The screen door burst open. Kevin strode outside sporting a grin like he'd just won the Irish Sweepstakes. He had one of Father Ted's weekend bags. "Hoooooly shit!" he cried. "Wait 'til you see this!" He dropped the canvas bag on the ground and squatted on his heels and unzipped the bag the rest of the way. Inside were thick stacks of magazines with unmistakably naked women on the covers. He reached in and drew one off the top. *Screw* magazine with a bare-assed, busty redhead looking back seductively from the cover.

"Whoa, check it out!" cried James. He hopped to his feet and drew a handful of magazines from the bag. "*Hustler! Club! Genesis! Penthouse!*" he cried.

Kevin flipped open a *Playboy* to the middle section and the centerfold dropped out like an attic ladder. "There's three more bags just like it."

That got James moving. He turned on his heels and ran inside, the screen door slapping behind him.

Kevin's eyes bulged in their sockets—to say nothing of the bulge in his jeans. "There's gotta be a hundred of these, at least," he said. He glanced at me, a quizzical look on his face. "You think he brought 'em for us?"

I didn't know what to say to that. I was still trying to make sense of it all. Only I couldn't. I had no frame of reference. No context. It was like running across an Eskimo in the Mojave Desert.

"They *gotta* be for us," Kevin said. "I mean, how many girlie magazines does one guy need?"

James returned with three more travel bags. "Check it out!" He drew out a stack of nudie magazines and plopped them on a milk crate. "Oh and there's more," he said. He reached into another bag and drew out a full liquor bottle.

Kevin studied the label. "Jim Beam. Kentucky Straight Bourbon Whiskey."

James went into the bag and drew out a bottle of Wild Turkey and two smaller pints. "Beefeater...and..." He studied the label. "*Smir*-noff."

"I don't think that's for us," I said. "He's getting us beer."

"There's enough liquor here to float the Queen Mary," Kevin said. "It can't all be for him."

I studied the bags. That was it for the booze, but at the bottom of one duffel was a plastic lunch bag containing what looked like oregano or thyme or some kind of spice.

James held up the baggie. "What have we here?"

Kevin snatched it away from him. He opened the bag and drew it to his nose and took a healthy sniff. Then he tossed the bag back to James. "It's pot, dumbass."

Pot? How did Kevin know what pot smells like? He didn't strike me as a pothead. And his dad was a cop. But somehow he knew.

My heart fluttered heavily up into my throat. Beer was one thing, pornography was another, but whiskey and dope…I wasn't prepared for that. I mean, pot was *illegal*. Sure, so was liquor if you were a minor, but pot was always illegal, no matter your age.

Anyway, the booze and the grass didn't hold our interest nearly as much as the magazines. When you're fifteen, nothing competes with naked ladies.

The three of us sat cross-legged around the pile of bags and flipped excitedly through the stacks of magazines. It felt like Christmas morning at the Playboy Mansion.

"Check out the pair on this one…"

"Man, I'd like to take a bite out of that ass!"

"Gimme some of them *Hustlers*, these *Playboys* suck."

I'd seen dirty magazines before, a few pages here and there, but nothing like this. Never this quantity. In fact, it was too much. My fifteen-year-old hormones were getting overloaded. I could feel a circuit about to blow. And I was embarrassed by the bulge in my pants which I tried to conceal by keeping a stack of magazines on my lap. As did Kevin and James.

After a while I got up and walked down the driveway until I came to the shot-up mailbox. For something to do, I counted the bullet holes. An even twenty. I scanned the highway for signs of the Jeep. The thing was, I didn't want Father Ted coming back and catching me going through his stuff. Maybe I was afraid he'd tell my uncle, the monsignor, who would then be obligated to tell my parents.

"Son, Monsignor tells us you got into Father Delaney's stash of booze, smut and dope. What have you got to say for yourself?"

"Uh—I repent?"

There was still no sign of the Jeep, so I drifted back to where James and Kevin sat with their boners, maniacally flipping through the magazines.

"Um, fellas?"

A thread of drool hung from Kevin's mouth. James's eyes glazed over as he flipped past Scotch whiskey ads and a lame story by the writer Norman Mailer.

"Guys, don't you think we ought to put this stuff away before Father Ted gets back?"

Kevin looked up and his face darkened. "Why? If it's okay for a priest to look at…"

I started to say something like, Yeah, but he's an *adult* priest. But that didn't make a whole lot of sense either.

None of it did.

James's look shifted to Kevin, then back to me, but he kept quiet. He didn't want to give up the magazines either.

I didn't know what else to do, so I hovered. I hovered until I succeeded in getting on Kevin's last nerve. Finally he sighed wearily and gave me a dark look. "Look, Doofus, if you're such a fag that you don't want to look at naked girls, you can be the lookout. Go stand by the road and holler when you see the Jeep coming."

I really wanted to punch Kevin in his stupid face. I didn't, though, because I knew it would be like punching a brick wall, and then that brick wall collapsing on top of me.

Kevin turned his head and said to James, "C'mon, let's take these inside." They collected the bags and carried them back into the house. "If a newly ordained priest has that much smut, imagine how much the pope must have!" I heard Kevin say before the screen door slammed behind him.

Like hell I'd be their lookout.

I glanced out across the county road. Dusk was seeping into the valley and soon the whole long, stupid day would be over. Then, only a day and a half to go.

I sat down on the cracked milk crate and fought the urge to feel sorry for myself. It was okay to feel anger, but never self-pity. Though what I mostly felt was confusion. I felt like a kid without a moral compass. Or a broken compass anyway.

I started thinking how the nuns who taught us Christian morals and values were always telling us how sinful everything was. Even prime-time TV shows like *Soap* and *M*A*S*H* were immoral. (Of course, we watched them anyway.) And at the same time you had priests chaperoning fifteen-year-old boys on various outdoor adventures with enough booze and dope and porn to last an entire rush week at a Florida university.

Was it any wonder I was confused?

Normally if I wasn't sure what the right thing was, I'd ask myself what my older brother or sister would do. (Never what my parents would do, since we were of very different generations, the key words being *very* and *different*.) Actually, my brother didn't have much of a moral compass either, so I usually went with my sister, even if she sometimes had too much compass, the way she'd police what I read or watched on TV. She certainly wouldn't have approved of Father Ted's dirty magazines or of him buying fifteen-year-olds alcohol. And pot? No way in hell. She would have thought that was crazy.

As I gazed blankly into the distance, the sound of excited voices carried through the one open window before dissipating on the evening air.

"Check the melons on this one!"

"Holy shit! I didn't know they grew 'em that big!"

What the hell was taking Father Ted and Dennis so long? They'd been gone over an hour.

I lifted my eyes as a tractor-trailer rumbled by on the lonely stretch of county road. The name OPIES was written on the side of the trailer and my thoughts skipped back to that old television show—the one with Andy and Barney and Goober and Floyd the Barber. I wondered how Sheriff Taylor and Deputy Fife would have made out in Iron Mountain, Missouri in the summer of 1978. Mayberry and Iron Mountain probably had a lot in common, both being white, southern mountain towns and county seats. As well as a few things not in common. Like Iron County's gangs of long-haired, drug-addled Vietnam vets.

It had gotten real quiet inside the ranch house. Kevin and James had probably slunk off somewhere to pull their puds. I went back to my book; it was no *Penthouse*, but it didn't make me feel like a degenerate either.

There was a loud squeal of tires. I glanced up to see the Jeep Wagoneer swerving crazily down the road, careening from side to side and kicking up waves of dirt and loose gravel as its tires skidded along the shoulder.

What the hell? That wasn't like Father Ted. He may have owned a sports car but he usually drove like an old woman. Maybe they'd gotten a head start on the booze? That would explain what had taken them so long.

The Jeep fishtailed and jerked and slowed to a crawl as it turned into the gravel drive. Then it slowly, ploddingly plowed into a scraggly, half-dead bush, and came to an abrupt halt. A cloud of dust rose up then drifted away on the wind. Over the idling engine a Donovan song droned:

Born high forever to fly…Wind velocity nil…

At first I didn't see anyone behind the wheel. Then I spied Dennis's crop of hay-colored hair sticking up above the dash. There was no one in the passenger seat.

What the hell was Dennis doing behind the wheel of the Jeep? And where was Father Ted?

I got to my feet for a closer look. Dennis was slouched in the driver's seat, a cigarette dangling from his lips and a bottle of beer wedged between his thighs. He was fiddling with the radio and didn't seem to notice me at all. I checked the back seat and the cargo area. There was no sign of Father Ted.

That's when I noticed it...that his shirt, his hair, his face, his hands, pretty much all of him was covered in...something. Something red and horrible. I felt a kind of panic deep in my bowels. I rapped on the window and Dennis slowly rolled his vacant eyes toward me.

"Roll down the window!" I shouted.

"Huh?"

"The window! Roll it down!"

Dennis snapped off the cassette player and rolled down the window.

"Holy shit, what happened to you?" I said. "Are you okay?"

Dennis raised the bottle to his lips and swallowed the last of the beer. Then he tossed the empty on the floorboards next to four other dead soldiers.

"Dennis, where's Father Ted?"

For a brief moment his gaze focused on me, then it drifted somewhere else.

"Dennis?"

He hiccuped. "Heeeeey Doofus!"

"Where's Father Ted?"

"Feather Tad?"

"Dennis!"

He lifted his finger to his lips as if to shush me. Then he leaned on the window and rested his chin on his bloodsplattered arms. "Lemme tell you a little secret," he said, slurring his words badly. "You know why they call you Doofus?"

"Dennis—"

"Give ya a hint. It ain't why you think."

I waited.

"It's 'cause you ain't real bright." He hiccupped and chuckled softly to himself. "No sir. Not real bright."

I glanced around for Kevin and James. Maybe they could get

some sense out of him. But wouldn't you know, they were still off pounding their puds somewhere.

I tried again. This time I nodded at his T-shirt. "Hey...is that blood?"

"This?" He plucked at his shirt. "Huh...some sticky-ass shit." Then he looked at me. "Don't worry, it's not mine."

His words had a vaguely familiar ring, though I couldn't place them at the time. I said, "Hey man, are you gonna tell me what happened?"

Dennis reached into a paper bag and drew out a bottle of beer. "You're a spiritual guy, ain't ya, Doofus? Gotta bunch of priests in your family?"

I fought to keep my voice steady. "Dennis, quit fucking around!"

"Any of them ever try anything funny? Any hanky-panky?"

Hanky-panky? What the hell was he talking about? Yeah, my uncle was a priest. A very stern, old-school, German-American priest. He was the antithesis of hanky panky.

"Lemme ask you something," Dennis said. "You kill a priest, you're going straight to hell, right? A one-way ticket? I mean, it's like a rule or something, right? What's it called...Mosaic Law?" He opened the driver's-side door and almost fell out. He propped an arm against the door and stood a moment weaving on his feet. "Where's Father Ted's Bible?"

Right then is where I'd say the bottom fell out for me. Right then is when I knew that this wasn't Dennis being crazy old freakshow Dennis, and that something really, really bad had happened. Right then is when I remembered what he had said the night before. That crack about *nobody dying tonight*. It was creepy then, but it was super fucking creepy now.

Dennis leaned on the door and twisted the cap off the beer bottle and tossed the cap over his shoulder. "I don't mean a good priest," he went on. "Not that I know any good priests...Maybe there aren't any." He gazed around and shook his head like he was looking for a way out of the crazy nightmare he'd stumbled into. "You know any good priests? What about your uncle? Is he a good guy? Seems like a Nazi to me. Sure sounds like a Nazi. 'Tell your *Fader* to get you *der Haarschnitt* for *der Faderland*!'"

I forced myself to breathe and then I cocked a thumb toward the house. "I'm just gonna go look for..."

Before I could go, however, Dennis stumbled over to the front steps and sat down, blocking the doorway. He drew the bottle to his lips and took a long swallow. "You ever read the Bible?" he said after a moment. "I mean *really* read it? I read it when I was nine, whole thing, cover to cover. My mom made me." He looked away. "Took me forever. Scared the bejeezus out of me. All them horror stories...floods and plagues and massacres and people turning into salt. And that freaky angel-of-death fucker." Dennis shivered at the memory, then he stared at me, unblinking. "You ever wonder why God made us?"

I slowly shook my head and took a few steps back. Maybe I'd try the back door.

"This one kid I knew at the group home, he used to say God likes to watch us fucking. That's why he did it. God is a big ol' pervert like that." Dennis laughed. "Interesting theory, but I don't think that's it." Shortly, out of a thoughtful silence, he said, "He ain't a pervert. He's a sadist. He likes to watch us *suffer*. He's like one of them kids that pulls the legs off bugs and watches them sink to the bottom of a puddle." He lifted his eyes at me. "You ever do that?"

I got my voice back somehow, though it sounded like a cat being strangled. "When you say *killed*...you mean like an accident? You got in an accident? Is that what happened?"

He wasn't listening. He leaned his head against the screen door and squeezed his eyes shut. Then he banged his head against the bottom aluminum panel. First slowly, then faster and faster. Harder and harder.

"Dennis! Hey! What're you doin'?"

BANG! BANG! BANG!

That's it, I thought. I am *not* qualified to deal with this level of craziness. I'm just going to quietly slip away…

The ruckus brought James and Kevin to the front door. "What's eating him?" Kevin said, scowling. "Hey, man, knock that shit off."

A worried look crept into James's eye. "Is that blood?"

Dennis paused a moment, then he cried, "I been washed in the blood, boys! Washed in the blood!"

They couldn't see what I could see. How Dennis was covered in gore from head to toe. Kevin tried to force open the screen door, but Dennis wouldn't budge.

"Hey, Dennis," Kevin said. "Move your ass."

Dennis didn't move.

Kevin's eyes scanned the front yard. "Where's Father Ted?"

I waited for Dennis to respond, to say Father Ted was dead or whatever he was going to say. Maybe say something crazy about God watching people having sex. But he didn't say a word.

"He says he's d-dead." My voice cracked into a thousand pieces on that last word. "I think. I mean…I'm not sure."

James grew visibly paler. "What?" he cried.

Kevin studied the top of Dennis's head. "Dennis, what the fuck's going on?"

Dennis looked at me but kept silent.

When I looked up again Kevin and James were gone.

Dennis took a swallow of beer and patted his empty trouser pockets. "What happened to my smokes?"

Kevin and James came tearing around the side of the house. When Kevin got a look at Dennis's blood-splattered clothes his mouth dropped open and he drew up short and James plowed into the back of him and down they went. Kevin angrily shoved James off of him and got to his feet. Then slowly, hesitantly, he approached Dennis.

"Hoooooly shit, what happened to you?"

Dennis rubbed his palms on the thighs of his threadbare jeans. "You ain't seen my smokes, have you?"

The three of us stared, dumbstruck. We were probably all having the same thoughts: He's insane—just like his uncle. And he's got a knife. Well, he had a knife. He might have several knives.

James and I withdrew a few steps. Then Kevin noticed we'd moved and he hurriedly joined us.

"Dennis, where's Father Ted?" Kevin said nervously, like he was speaking to a third-grader sucking on a live grenade.

James said, "And why are you covered in blood?"

"I already asked him that," I said.

"Come on, man, this is serious," Kevin said. "Where is Father Ted?"

Dennis slowly lifted his head. His eyes had taken on a dead, vacant look, as if they'd been disconnected from the rest of him. "*I'm just mad about fourteeeen,*" he sang in a eerie voice. "*Fourteen's mad about me.*"

Kevin, James and I shared a look of absolute dread.

"Stop fucking around!" Kevin cried. "I'm gonna ask you one more time—"

The question—or maybe its tone—seemed to irritate Dennis. Anger sparked in his eyes and he turned and waved a bloody hand toward the highway. "Back there somewhere! I don't know!"

Kevin swallowed, then his eyes shifted to me and James and he nodded toward the Jeep like he wanted us to huddle over there. The three of us went around to the back of the Jeep, out of earshot.

"What the fuck's going on?" Kevin hissed at me.

"How should I know?" I cried. "All I know is...he's saying Father Ted's dead...Maybe they got in a car accident."

"Dead? Did he say that?"

"Yes! I mean...I don't know!"

"What do you mean you don't know?"

"I don't know! What do you want me to say?"

Dennis called out, "Hey, be a dear and bring me a beer!"

Kevin seized James by the arm and drew him close. "You're his cousin. You talk to him."

James looked like he swallowed a frog. He glanced uneasily toward Dennis. "What am I supposed to ask him?"

"Find out what happened!"

James drew a breath, then he opened the car door and grabbed a bottle of beer out of the front seat. He went over to where Dennis sat, eyes closed, legs stretched before him, his head resting against the screen door.

Kevin and I followed at a safe distance.

James handed Dennis the bottle. "Dennis, what the hell happened? Did you and Father Ted get in a car accident or something?"

Dennis glanced up at his cousin. His eyes wavered like they'd gone out of focus and got stuck that way. "Noooooo," he said.

"Well that's good." James paused. "So…what happened?"

At that moment something venomous seemed to creep into Dennis's eyes as they went narrow and dark. "What happened? You wanna know what happened? I'll tell you what happened," he said. "I stabbed the motherfucker."

LOOKING BACK, I don't think any of us really believed that Dennis could have done something so horrible, something so unimaginable—even though we knew he was nuts and came from a family of psychopaths. Not even with all the blood evidence staring us in the face. It was too far out of the realm of possibility to a bunch of naive, fifteen-year-old Catholic school kids. It was more the stuff of R-rated movies, which I wasn't even allowed to watch.

A long, slow moment ticked by. I stood there trying to get my breath evened out while we waited for Dennis to say something else, to hopefully start busting up, tell us he sure got us good that time. That it was all just one of his crazy, elaborate put-ons.

I waited until I couldn't wait any more, then I asked him outright. "You're joking, right? This is one of your stupid jokes?"

Dennis seemed to think about that, then he snorted. "Now that would be funny, wouldn't it?" He looked thoughtful again and his smile widened.

I shivered inside—not from the cold—more like from the icy jab of Death's bony finger.

He wasn't joking. There hadn't been an accident. That only left one possibility that I could see. And I did not want to think about that.

James muttered, "This can't be real."

Kevin peered at Dennis for a while. His eyes were like dark, swirling clouds of confusion. "Why?" he cried. "Why would you do that?"

Dennis slowly lifted his gaze and got to his feet. "If anybody deserved it, he did." He strode over to the Jeep and grabbed a pack of cigarettes off the dash and one of the brown grocery bags. "Think I'll put these on ice." Then he went inside.

The three of us stood in stunned silence.

Today, a fifteen-year-old would immediately pull out his smartphone and call his parents. Or dial 911. And just like that the whole thorny ethical dilemma would have been put behind him. Or at least taken out of his hands. No back and forth, no moral quandaries, no fistfights, no negotiations, no cover up. But in those days, in the middle of nowhere, our options were, you might say, limited.

A sharp wind ruffled James's hair. He shifted on his feet and said, "What do we do now?"

I turned to look at Kevin…he usually had all the answers. The wrong answers, sure. But this time he didn't even seem to have those.

I steeled myself and said, "You don't really believe he—"

"How the hell would I know?" Kevin snapped.

James wet his lips, uneasily. "Guys, we gotta go look for

him. What if he's out there somewhere? What if—"

"Look where?" Kevin said. "You heard what that nutjob said. He doesn't know where he is. He could be anywhere!"

I felt my face grow hot and the cords in my neck tightened. "So what do you wanna do, sit around here and beat off 'til somebody sends out a rescue party?"

Kevin balled his fist and gave me a death stare, but he held off clobbering me...for now anyway. "It's gonna be dark in a few minutes and none of us got a driver's license," he said. "You wanna drive up and down the backroads of Iron County at night looking for a dead body?"

"No," I said, "I wanna call the sheriff!"

"Call him how?" Kevin nodded toward the house. "Did you see a phone in there?"

"So we drive into town, to the sheriff's office."

"And what do we tell them? We don't even know what happened! And you think Dennis is gonna just walk into the police station and turn himself in?"

"I don't care what *he* does, but we gotta tell somebody!"

James cried, "Guys, we gotta go look for Father Ted!"

I glared at James. "No, we tell the sheriff and let him find Father Ted!"

At that moment Dennis strode outside with a pint of bourbon in one hand and a dirty magazine in the other. He had put on a new T-shirt and scrubbed some of the blood off his arms and hands and face. "This sure beats that shitty beer," he said and turned up the bottle and bubbled it several times. He sputtered and coughed. "Did you get a load of those bags full of dirty magazines?" Then he held out the pint and shook it at us. "Who wants a belt?"

"This ain't the time," Kevin said.

"*Au contraire*. There's never been a better time."

I drew Kevin aside. Of the three of us, he was the only one who wasn't the least bit intimidated by Dennis. "Talk to him," I said. "Find out where Father Ted is."

Kevin glared at me. "*You* talk to him."

Dennis wiped his mouth with the back of his hand. "What do you wanna talk about?" A moment passed as he studied us one by one. "Fellas, I'm not stupid. I know what you're thinking."

Kevin smiled coldly. "Yeah? What are we thinking?"

"You're thinking about my uncle."

We were—at least I was—but I wasn't about to say so.

Dennis went on, "Well, you can stop."

"And why's that?" Kevin said.

"Because this was different. I had to. I didn't have a choice." He took a breath. "It was self-defense." Dennis's gaze fell on us one by one. He must have read something dismaying in our faces because his look turned suddenly to one of profound disappointment. "You don't believe me?"

"Self-defense?" Kevin said. "What are you saying...Father Ted tried to kill you?"

Dennis thought about that. "Worse."

What the fuck could be worse? I thought.

It got real quiet then. Dennis let out a deep breath and his shoulders seemed to slump. Then he turned and looked away from us. "Eh, what's the use...no one's gonna believe me."

"How do you know?" Kevin said. "Maybe if you'd tell us what the hell happened? The truth!"

"I already told you," Dennis said through his teeth. "I had to!"

Kevin said, "But *why*? What did he do to you?"

If Dennis hadn't been covered in blood, I wouldn't have suspected anything had happened to him. There wasn't a scratch on him.

Dennis shut his eyes and turned away again. "I'm done talking about it."

"What?" Kevin cried. "What do you mean you're done? You just told us you stabbed Father Ted! You better fucking believe you're gonna talk about it!"

Dennis shook his head. "What's the point?" He took a pull on the bourbon and shifted uneasily. "Who's gonna believe me?"

I was starting to think he was right. That we wouldn't believe him, no matter what he said. And if *we* didn't believe him, who the hell would?

Nobody, that's who.

Then James said, "Can you at least tell us where he is?"

Dennis hesitated. "Why?"

"So we can see if he's still alive!"

"Trust me, he ain't."

"We need to make sure!"

For a moment Dennis looked impassively into the distance, then he took a hit off the bottle and wiped his mouth with the back of his hand. "Morbid sonsabitches." He shrugged his shoulders. "Okay. Sure. Let's go for a little evening drive in the country. But all I know is he's somewhere between here and town, down some lonesome dirt road."

James asked us to wait while he ran inside to fetch his flashlight. Once an Eagle Scout, always an Eagle Scout, I guess. A moment later he came back with an old chrome flashlight that looked like it had belonged to someone's great-grandfather. He tested the light and it sort of worked.

"Ready," James said.

"I got my permit so I'm driving," Kevin said.

Dennis said, "Permit don't mean shit without an adult."

Kevin snapped his fingers at Dennis. "Keys!" he said.

Dennis hiccuped. "They're in the Jeep."

We climbed into the Wagoneer, Kevin and Dennis in front, James and me in the back. We waited anxiously to see if Kevin knew what he was doing behind the wheel. He wiped the sweat off his upper lip and slid the key into the ignition. The Jeep rumbled to life. He jammed the gearshift into drive. The easy part was over. He didn't even try to back up, just made a long, jerky swing through the rutted, trash-strewn front yard until the

Jeep bumped onto the county road. He took it slow and easy, his hands forming a death grip on the steering wheel, his gaze glued to the two-lane blacktop.

Every so often Kevin would ask Dennis if he recognized anything, and Dennis would respond with a smart-ass comment like, "We're looking for a rock that looks like a bear...or is it a bear that looks like a rock?" Then he'd go back to pulling on the bourbon and flipping through the *Penthouse*.

"Will you put that fucking thing down and keep your eyes out the window!" Kevin snapped.

Dennis sighed and tossed the magazine on top of the dashboard and stared moodily out the passenger-side window.

The sun had dipped below the ridgeline and the countryside lay in deep shadows, darker than a Kentucky murder ballad. An evening chill had settled down in the valley and we turned off the air conditioner and rolled down the windows. The fresh cool air came like a second wind. Kevin turned on the headlights. Dennis turned on the radio. Kevin snapped off the radio and warned Dennis not to touch it again.

For a good half hour we rolled up and down Highway 72. As dusk came on we took to the backroads. Old Chicken Farm Road. Shepherd Mountain Road. Middlebrook Road. We skirted a weedy, long-forgotten cemetery and a field of sorghum and a dried-up creek bed flanked by dogwoods and river birches. An old red International Harvester pickup rambled past. The anonymous driver honked and waved and tossed an empty beer can in his wake.

"Pull over," Dennis said.

"You see it?" James said.

"I think I'm gonna barf."

Kevin pulled over to the shoulder and Dennis thrust his head out the window and made a sick moaning sound and spat into the gravel a few times, but nothing substantial came up. He seemed genuinely disappointed. He wiped his mouth with his hand. "False alarm."

We drove on. A moment passed. "You don't have a fucking clue where he is," Kevin grumbled.

Dennis leaned his head out the window, the wind ruffling his curly mop. He seemed to be studying something. I glanced out the window and spied a kettle of turkey vultures circling lazily against the amber evening clouds.

"Maybe not, but I bet they do," Dennis said.

The birds turned lazily over a crop field a few hundred yards to the north. As I watched an icy wind blew up my spine.

"Slow down," Dennis said.

"Is this it?" Kevin said.

"Maybe," Dennis said. "There oughta be a little tractor lane that runs off into a cornfield and this little ol' falling-down bridge."

"What the hell were you doing out here?" Kevin said.

Dennis pushed in the cigarette lighter and shook a smoke from a pack on the dash. "Wasn't my idea."

We drove on again. Kevin muttered something under his breath. James chewed his fingernail. Dennis smoked and took hits off the pint bottle. And I studied the darkening landscape. I didn't see any roads or bridges. Only soybean and sorghum fields and a dry creek and a sad tumbledown barn. "This looks like every place we've been for the past half hour," I said.

"Just keep heading toward them dudes," Dennis said. He grew solemn and gazed ahead at the redheaded vultures. "You know what this reminds me of? That verse from Matthew. *And when the wise men saw the buzzards they were filled with joy.*"

"Jesus Christ on a cracker," Kevin said.

Another pickup passed and honked.

Dennis leaned forward and pointed. "Slow down now," he said. "There...turn there." Ahead of us lay the entrance to an overgrown tractor lane. And just down the road sat a small wooden bridge.

Dennis's face broke into a wide snaggle-toothed grin. "We found it," he said. "I honestly didn't think we would." Then he slouched back in his seat and took a final drag on his smoke and flicked the butt out the window. "My bet is y'all gonna wish we didn't."

CHAPTER 5

THE LITTLE TRUSS bridge spanned a stillwater creek that ran through a field of dent corn before winding its way adjacent to the dirt road. The bridge had been built to carry tractors back when tractors were a quarter of the size they are now; these days the bridge probably couldn't support more than a couple of riding lawnmowers. From one of the trusses hung a NO TRESPASSING sign pockmarked with #4 shot. A quarter of the boards on the bridge were cracked or missing. I sure hoped they weren't the important ones.

The evening still held a pinch of light, which tinted the sky amber and deep blue amid splotches of long black clouds. Down in the corn, however, everything beyond the spray of headlights shaded to degrees of gray. We drove slowly on, the walls of corn closing in on both sides until you couldn't help but feel claustrophobic. We came to a stop at the bridge. I eyed Kevin warily. Large beads of sweat stood out on his forehead. "This don't look real safe," he said and rubbed his upper lip with his knuckles.

"I been across it twice and it ain't fell in yet," Dennis said.

It got real quiet inside the Jeep as the four of us envisioned the bridge collapsing (in slow motion) beneath us.

"How far is he?" I said. "Maybe we should get out and walk."

"It's still a good hike," Dennis said. "Keep driving."

James opened his door and the overhead light blinked on. "I'm getting out while you cross the bridge."

Kevin pumped the brakes. "Get your ass back in here. If one of us goes down, we all go down."

"How does that make any sense?" James said.

"Shut the door!" Kevin snapped.

James swore under his breath and slammed the door shut and fell back in his seat. I didn't think we'd be killed if the bridge collapsed. It probably wasn't more than a ten-foot drop. At most we'd get banged up some: a few broken bones, a punctured lung. Getting to a hospital would be the hard part.

I held onto my breath as we rumbled over the warped, weathered boards. Time seemed to slow down like it tends to do when you want it to speed up. When the rear tires finally made contact with the dirt road, the four of us let out a loud, collective sigh of relief.

"Nice driving, Slick," Dennis said.

Soon the wall of corn gave way on one side to a large thicket of tall, ghostly white trees that flanked the long creek bend.

"I don't see him," Kevin said. Then he hit the brights. "Wait…"

Up ahead something momentarily gleamed and was gone. The yellow eyes of a coyote or a bobcat or, God help us, some kind of unholy demon.

Then we saw him. Kevin jammed the gear shift into park and we sat there for a long moment, staring silently up the road as the engine hummed and ticked and clouds of moths and beetles danced in our headlights.

"Wanna belt first?" Dennis said, offering the bottle around.

No one replied.

"In that case I'll let you fellas take it from here," he said. "But we'll be here if you need us. Me and ol' Jimmy Beam."

Kevin opened the driver's-side door. "Bring the flashlight," he told James. Then his iron gaze fell on me. "Let's go, Doofus."

There was no point in arguing. I eased out of the Jeep and the three of us crept forward slowly, hesitantly, our bodies blocking out the light from the headlights. As we drew closer, plodding shoulder to shoulder, my blood pounded in my ears so loudly it drowned out the evening bug broadcast. James kept the flashlight focused on the ground a few steps ahead of us, like he was in no hurry to see whatever lay ahead.

Some fifteen yards away we halted in our tracks. He lay in the dust with his backside to us, dead still.

I went cold all over and my scrotum shriveled up to the size of a peanut.

"Hoooooly shit," James whispered.

That was my first thought too. Maybe my second and third thoughts too. My fourth thought was: *He just left him lying in the road...like a piece of roadkill.*

"Gimme the flashlight," Kevin said. He shone the light up ahead. In the dim spray of light I began to make out things. Horrible, ghastly things. Things I would never be able to unsee. Things that would haunt my dreams for the rest of my life.

It was him, all right. No mistake. The same white-and-blue striped beach shirt and the white Bermuda shorts he'd had on that morning. Only they weren't white any more.

I stared in silent horror as my whole body seemed to shake like a wet dog.

Kevin cocked his head toward the body. "Go see if he's got a pulse."

"Not me," James said.

Kevin fixed his eyes on me, but I was unable to respond. I couldn't even shake my head. I was all frozen up, inside and out.

"Go on, Doofus!"

That snapped me out of it. "I don't know how," I said. It was true. I'd seen it done on TV shows, but that wasn't real life.

"Useless," Kevin said. "Bunch of useless pussies." He slapped at something on the back of his neck and wiped his palm on his pant leg. "C'mon," he said.

We all went then, slowly creeping up on Father Ted, ready in case he sprang to his feet or something crazy. You never could tell with holy men and women. They can do strange and mystical things, especially the ones that are saints. Some of them, like Christina the Astonishing, could come back to life and throw themselves into burning furnaces for hours without suffering a single burn. And some could fly or be in two places at the same time. Or so we were told in religion class.

Kevin handed me the flashlight. I didn't want it. I tried to give it to James, but he wouldn't take it.

Kevin squatted beside Father Ted. I tried not to look.

"Shine it on *him*, Doofus, not the road! Jesus!"

The light kept fading in and out. I smacked the flashlight with the heel of my palm and it started working again. I squatted beside Kevin. The light illuminated Father Ted's face.

His eyes were open.

I let out a wild animal scream and dropped the flashlight and scrambled backwards on my hands and feet, knocking heads with James.

"Son of a bitch!" James cried.

"What?" Kevin said.

"He's alive!" I cried.

"What are you talking about?"

"His eyes are open!"

Kevin picked up the flashlight and the light touched Father Ted's face. He drew in a sharp breath. "Yeah, well people die with their eyes open. Don't you know anything?"

I stared, dumbstruck. I don't know why I was so freaked out at the thought of Father Ted being alive, but I was. I guess I hadn't prepared for that possibility.

Not that he *was* alive...

I got to my feet and massaged the rising knot on the back of my head.

Dennis suddenly called out to us: "He had a bag of pot on him. In his front pocket. You might wanna retrieve that." He'd gotten out of the Jeep and was now sitting against the front tire having a cigarette.

Kevin glanced up at me and James, like, *Can you believe this guy?* Then he took a deep breath and leaned over and put two fingers on Father Ted's neck.

"Anything?" James said.

Kevin slowly shook his head. "He's fucking cold." Kevin had gotten blood on his fingers and he wiped them on his pant leg. Then he glanced up at us with eyes that looked red-rimmed and wet. It was the first sign of emotion—besides anger—that he'd shown since we'd left home.

A moment passed, then Kevin shook his head and got to his feet. "Well, he wasn't lying."

"You're sure?" I said.

"What...that he's dead? What do you want, a fucking death certificate?" He turned and strode back to the Jeep. James gave me a blank look and turned and followed him.

"So now what do we do?" James said.

"How the fuck do I know?" Kevin said.

One of the buzzards glided down and perched atop the bridge and watched us with red stoic eyes. Kevin, meanwhile, leaned over and started to say something to Dennis—I couldn't hear what—when Dennis suddenly shifted to his hands and knees and started sputtering and retching. He groaned and his back arched and up came a few quarts of vomit, exploding out his mouth like water from a fire hydrant.

"WOOOOOOLAAAAAAAA!"

It seemed like it would never end. I went over and slammed down the tailgate and sat there feeling my insides hardening like concrete. After a moment James joined me. He looked like he was having a hard time keeping it together.

"WOOOOOOLAAAAAAAA!"

Dennis' stomach must have been running on empty, because nothing was coming up but those horrible wounded-buffalo sounds.

JACKS FORK

Eventually Kevin drifted over and sat down beside us. "We gotta get that booze away from that idiot."

I didn't like the sound of that. It sounded dangerous and unnecessarily provocative. Just let him get drunk. Who cares? "Wouldn't we be better off if we let him drink until he passes out?" I said.

"And what if he don't pass out? He just threw up everything he drank for the past two hours."

I didn't know what to say to that. I just wanted to hand this nightmare off to an adult. Any functioning adult would do. I wasn't particular.

Kevin said, "I'm tired of babysitting that fucking psycho. We're getting rid of that bottle. All the bottles." He glanced at Dennis, then his gaze shifted to me for a moment.

I braced myself for more bad news.

"I'll distract him while you get the bottle and toss it into the woods." He hesitated. "And don't let him see you." He turned and studied Dennis for a moment. "We gotta do it now, while he's still barfing."

Actually we don't, I thought. I could think of two dozen other things we *had to do,* or *should do,* but tossing Dennis's whiskey into the woods was not one of them. But, for whatever reason, I was not the one calling the shots.

Kevin strode up to Dennis and squatted down next to him and his puddle of puke. Reluctantly, I got off the tailgate and quietly slipped in behind them. The bottle of Jim Beam lay on its side in the dirt. There was maybe a quarter of a bottle remaining, if that.

"WHOOOOOOLAAAAAAAA!"

"That's right, buddy, get it *all* up," Kevin said, his voice oozing with fake concern. He glanced at me and his eyes darted toward the whiskey bottle. My signal. I scooped up the bottle, backpedaled a few steps, spun, and let it fly. I damn near threw my arm out of its socket. It was a good toss, though. It sailed in a long, high arc and crashed into a stand of birch trees. The bottle collided with a branch and shattered.

LOUD.

It got real quiet then. I stood stock still and waited for all hell to break loose.

Only Dennis hadn't heard a thing. He sat in the middle of the road, his feet spread out before him, wiping his mouth on his shirt and spitting in the dust. "I should've stayed home," he said.

"We all should have stayed home," James said.

Kevin gave Dennis a few consoling pats on the shoulder. "Feelin' better, pal?"

Dennis let out a long, sickly groan. I went back and sat on the tailgate next to James. Out on the county road a pair of Harleys thundered past. After the noise died down, James said, "So now what do we do?"

Kevin whirled on him sharply. "Will you stop asking that! Jesus! Just shut the hell up so I can think!"

Dennis spat into the dust and muttered something I couldn't hear.

"What'd he say?" Kevin said.

Dennis made a face like he had bitten into something rotten. "Bury the sumbitch."

We all looked at each other for a second. "Are you fucking mad?" I said. I waited a moment for Kevin and James to back me up, but of course they didn't. "We gotta call an ambulance!"

"What good would that do?" Kevin said. "It's too late for an ambulance."

"Well we gotta call somebody!"

"No shit, Sherlock!" Kevin cried, then his face knotted in thought. A long moment went by. "I know who we could call. My dad's a cop. He'll know what to do."

Dennis studied the vomit between his legs like it was some kind of abstract expressionist masterpiece he couldn't interpret. Then he snorted up a large quantity of phlegm. "We ain't callin'…we ain't callin' nobody."

Kevin turned and laid his eyes on Dennis. "Your crazy drunk ass ain't in charge here."

For that one brief moment, Kevin was something like a hero to me. Of course, it couldn't last. Suddenly his gaze shifted to the little truss bridge where there were now three vultures observing us, then his eyes focused back on James. "Who thinks we ought to call my dad?"

James shrugged noncommittally. I don't know what I would have said if he had asked me. Kevin's dad was a bigger asshole than he was. But still, he was a cop. A dirty one. He probably would have known what to do.

Dennis cried, "I did it, I get to decide!"

Kevin folded his arms. "Oh, so that's how this works."

"Damn straight!"

A tractor trailer rumbled down the county road and I followed it with my eyes until I lost it behind a row of timber. God, how I envied that driver, rolling down the highway, sipping coffee, chewing tobacco, listening to Merle Haggard, popping a few pills to stay awake. Soon he'd be a hundred miles from here, the lucky bastard.

Kevin said, "I'll tell you one thing. We ain't burying nobody. At least I ain't. You want to bury him, go ahead. But you're on your own. I ain't helping. I ain't being an accessory."

"'Cessory?" Dennis said. "'Cessory to what?"

"What do you think?"

Dennis looked squarely at Kevin. "I told you it was self-defense!"

"Yeah, but you ain't told us why!"

Dennis squared himself but did not answer.

Kevin said, "Dennis, we've all seen him! We all saw what you did to him!"

Dennis's look skipped along the ground. "Where's my bottle?"

Nobody said anything.

"Where's my fucking—"

He lunged at Kevin, but Kevin nimbly sidestepped his grasp.

"What'd you do with it?" Dennis said.

"I didn't touch it."

Dennis put his eyes on me. The look was vicious, terrible, but he didn't say anything more about the bourbon. Instead he turned back to Kevin. "Okay," he said. "You wanna know what happened? You really wanna know?"

We waited.

Dennis's eyes flashed out at us. "What do you think we were doing out here? Collectin' butterflies?"

Kevin gave Dennis a hard stare. "No idea."

"No idea." Dennis laughed bitterly. "Buncha fuckin' Boy Scouts." He locked eyes with Kevin. "Do I gotta draw ya a picture?"

I wished he would draw a picture, or at least an outline, because I had no clue what Dennis was getting at. I don't think anyone else did either.

A soft red glow from the taillights settled on the dust where Dennis sat hugging his legs with his arms, rocking slightly. "You really don't have a clue, do ya? None of you." His eyes flared up again, then almost instantly the light went out. "The bastard tried to bugger me."

His words hung heavily in the air for a minute. I glanced at James. He sucked in his cheeks and stared hard into the darkness.

"That plain enough? Or do I have to explain that, too?"

It might have been plain enough for Kevin and James, but not for me. *Bugger* was not a term I was familiar with. I figured it must be bad though, real bad...bad enough to knife someone over.

I'll admit, for a fifteen-year-old I was incredibly naive. Then again, this was the late Seventies in the tip of the Bible Belt. People didn't talk about such things. Or maybe they did. Like I said, I didn't have many friends, so who knows what other kids talked about. It sure wasn't all over TV and the Internet like it is now. What can I say? Buggering was light years beyond what I could comprehend.

What Dennis said next stopped me cold.

"What would you have done? Let him butt-shank you...or do what I did?"

The wind rushed out of my lungs and I felt my knees buckle.

So...I now had a better idea what *bugger* meant. Not a complete picture. More like a detail. But that detail freaked the shit out of me.

Kevin's gaze shifted to me and James. "Who's got the flashlight?"

I tossed Kevin the flashlight, happy to be rid of it. He went over to where Father Ted lay and ran the light over him for a few seconds. He let out a long deep breath. "Jesus, man, how many times did you stab him?"

Dennis slowly got to his feet. He walked unsteadily to the front of the Jeep and leaned against the hood and studied Father Ted's lifeless corpse. He shook his head slowly. "He wouldn't quit. He just kept coming at me, no matter how many times I stuck him. Like he was possessed. He wouldn't stop." He paused and wiped his nose with the back of his hand. "What was I gonna do? He wouldn't...fuckin'...die..."

It was my turn to vomit. I staggered to the side of the road and fell on my hands and knees and tossed up everything I had inside me. Then I moved on to the dry heaves. Afterward, I sat on my ass in the dust and took big gulps of air and waited for my stomach to settle and my throat to stop burning. The whole time Dennis's words kept ringing in my ears: *"He wouldn't...fuckin'...die..."*

I didn't know what to think. My mind was spinning like a runaway carousel. Back then my natural disposition was to assume the best in other people, be they priests or football coaches or Boy Scout leaders or the creepy, tattooed gun collector who lived with his mother in the double-wide down the street. I've grown a lot more cynical over the years, but at the time I really wanted to believe Dennis, that what he said about it being self-defense was the truth. At the same time I wanted to believe that Father Ted was basically a good guy. Bags of pot and skin magazines and gallons of alcohol to the contrary.

I wiped the vomit off my lips with my T-shirt and went back to sit on the tailgate. What I wouldn't have given for a swig of that bourbon I'd just tossed into the woods.

James sobbed, "I want to go home."

Suddenly Dennis hopped up on the tailgate. Then, with the deftness of a tree squirrel, he scrambled up to the roof of the Jeep and perched there. "We're here," he said. "We might as well bury him."

I turned and glared at Dennis. "We are *not* gonna do that!"

For once Kevin agreed with me. "Doofus's right. Why would we do that? You just said it was self-defense."

"Except who's gonna believe me? You guys don't even believe me."

Kevin said, "I never said I didn't believe you."

"Use your head. He's a priest. You think these backwoods Baptists down here are gonna take the word of someone like me—a punk who's spent half his life in group homes? And wait 'til they find out who my uncle is."

I stared fixedly at my shoes, my mind moving in a dozen different directions. I hadn't known about the group homes, but I can't say I was surprised. It certainly wasn't helping his case any.

"They're gonna say I'm evil or possessed," Dennis said. "Just like they said about my uncle."

Possessed? I thought. Like in *The Exorcist?* That girl played by Linda Blair...didn't she kill a priest too? Didn't she hurl his ass out a window? Or did the priest fling *himself* out the window? I couldn't remember. Whatever the case, this was not the kind of decision that a bunch of clueless teenagers should be making. *You want ketchup on your hot dog?* maybe. But not this.

For a long time nobody said anything. Deep down we must have known that whatever we said or did at that moment was going to have profound, long-term effects on our future, and nobody wanted to be the one to fuck up our future.

But we couldn't just sit there all night not saying or doing anything.

It was James who finally broke the silence. He said, "I believe you, Dennis."

Dennis regarded him coolly. "Why? Did he try something with you?"

"No," James said, sounding slightly offended. "I...I just believe you. I mean, him bringing us down here...the pot and the magazines and all that booze. What else could it mean?" His gaze shifted to Kevin. "That's why I think we ought to call your dad."

"No way," Dennis said. "No fucking way are we telling a cop. Any cop. No way am I gonna be locked up for life. Not for stabbing a child molester."

"They don't lock you up for self-defense!" I said.

"What the fuck do you know about it? How many times have you been in jail?"

None, I thought. Like most normal people!

It got real quiet again, then a light seemed to go on behind Dennis's eyes. "The only way I'll agree to that is if you guys say he did it to you too."

Kevin and James and I shared a pained look.

"But he didn't," I said. "Not me, anyway."

"Man, that doesn't make any sense," Kevin said. "We're supposed to lie and say he tried to rape us?"

"Not tried."

"Are you nuts?" Kevin cried. "I'm not saying that!"

I shook my head too. James studied his shoelaces.

"I guess we're burying him then," Dennis said.

"I ain't burying nobody!" I said.

Dennis sprang from the roof of the Jeep and bounded off the

tailgate like it was a diving board. He planted himself in front of me and seized hold of my T-shirt and pulled me down toward him. For a scrawny little guy, he was surprisingly strong. He drew me toward him until our noses were about an inch apart. His eyes were glassy and hard, his breath hot and sour and smelling of booze and vomit. "You listen to me, Doofus. We're all in this together, ya hear? He could just as easily have taken you out here and tried to bugger you, only you—"

I hauled off and clipped Dennis with a roundhouse that landed flat on his ear. The blow sent him sprawling. He lost his balance and stumbled backwards and dropped on his ass in the drainage ditch. (I'm sure if I had thought about it I wouldn't have swung at him, considering he'd already stabbed one person to death that day.) Dennis picked himself up and shot out after me, eyes ablaze. I half expected him to draw a pocketknife and make like I was Janet Leigh in a Bates Motel shower. Thank God he didn't. Maybe he though a knife would be excessive.

It was Kevin who saved my neck. He slipped behind Dennis and put the squeeze on him, lifting him entirely off the ground, Dennis's feet kicking comically in mid-air.

"Cut the crap!" Kevin shouted.

"Let go of me or I'll kill ya!"

"I will if you cool it!"

Dennis slowly wound down like a cheap mechanical toy. "Okay!" he shouted.

Kevin held him a few seconds longer and then released him. Dennis dropped to his feet. He staggered down the road a short distance, then he stopped and drew himself up and hitched up his trousers. A long moment ticked by before he shuffled back, head down, hands jammed in his pockets, kicking at the dirt. "I didn't mean that—" His voice had grown steady now. He sounded genuinely sorry, though I suspected it was all an act and he was preparing for a counter-attack.

For the first time ever I was glad that Kevin Przybysz was

around and that he was a hundred and fifty-five pounds of muscle and bone.

"Forget it," I said. I shuffled away down the road out of harm's way and promising myself to keep one eye on Dennis Hailey at all times.

After the way he handled Dennis, Kevin must have decided he was officially in charge, that he was now our undisputed leader, and that whatever he said goes. No one ever came to it more naturally.

"All right," he said. "Here's what we're gonna do—and if any of you don't like it, too fucking bad." He drew a long breath and slowly let it out. "We're gonna drive back to Danny's uncle's house—"

"Wait," James said.

"And just leave him?" I said.

"He ain't going anywhere!" Kevin cried. "Look, we need to take some time and think about this, what we're gonna do. We can decide in the morning." Here he glanced at Dennis. "When everyone's sober and thinking clearly." After a pause he continued, "Maybe things will look different in the morning."

"Why would anything look different?" I said. "Nothing's gonna change overnight. Unless someone finds him out here."

Kevin put his eyes on me flat and hard. "We are not debating this."

"Who the hell died and made you pope?" I said. I was still riding an adrenaline high from punching Dennis, so my brain wasn't exactly calling the shots.

Before Kevin could respond verbally or physically, James spoke up. "What are we supposed to do, leave him lying in the middle of the road? What if someone comes along—"

"Nobody's coming out here…"

James said, "I'd say there's been a hell of a lot of traffic out here today."

"Fine!" Kevin said. "We'll move him out of the road."

"If we're gonna do that, why not just bury him?" Dennis said.

"Because we ain't got a goddamn shovel, for one thing!" Kevin turned and looked at me steadily. Then his head jerked a little, nodding toward Father Ted. "You and James get his legs."

What the hell?" I said. "What happened to you not wanting to be an accessory?"

"We're just gonna move him outta the road! Now get his legs."

I hesitated. I knew the second I touched that corpse I might as well start digging my own grave.

Only it was three against one.

"What about him?" I said, nodding at Dennis. "Why isn't he helping?"

Kevin tossed him the flashlight, which Dennis fumbled and nearly dropped.

"Shine the light ahead of us," Kevin said.

"Aye, aye, Captain!" Dennis saluted and turned on the flashlight. He held it to his mouth like a microphone. "Hello, is this thing on?"

Kevin shook his head, then he squared himself and set his jaw. "Let's do this."

I really, really, really did not want to help them. But you know how peer pressure can be. Especially when one of your peers just stabbed a man to death.

Besides, I wanted to get the hell out of there before someone came along and saw us and we all ended up spending the rest of summer in the Iron County Jailhouse.

That pretty much explains why I went along.

James and I grabbed Father Ted's ankles and Kevin lifted him under the arms. He was not a light man when he was alive, so the deadweight was like moving a couple of pianos. I kept my gaze averted so I wouldn't have to look at him. I couldn't stand that. We followed Dennis into a thicket, far enough in so he couldn't be seen from the road, and when we came to a small clearing we set him down gently on his back.

We stood looking at each other over Father Ted's corpse.

"We're really gonna do this?" I said. "Just leave him out here alone?"

Kevin looked at me contemptuously. "Feel free to stay out here and keep him company," he said. Then he turned and walked back to the Jeep.

That's where we left him. It felt wrong, him being a priest and all, leaving him out there for the wild animals and buzzards to get at. Then again it was going to feel wrong no matter what we did.

CHAPTER 6

THE NEXT MORNING I found Kevin scrubbing bloodstains off the front seats of the Jeep Wagoneer. He looked tanned and rested in cut-offs and a clean sleeveless T-shirt. I hadn't slept more than two hours. Kevin had rustled up a tin bucket and some chewed-up dishrags and was using both arms to aggressively attack the bloodstains.

He said, "About time you got up." His face puckered to a scowl. "This shit don't want to come off. We're gonna need some industrial-strength cleaning supplies."

That seemed like a bad sign to me, a sign that he'd already made up his mind. That we were going to flee the scene of the crime and hope nobody stumbled on the body—at least until we got back to St. Louis.

"You know that's evidence," I said, in the most non-whiny voice I could muster.

"Not any more, it ain't."

I felt my face get hot. "You know destroying evidence is a serious crime."

Kevin wrung out the dishrag over the bucket. The water was a sickly, gray-pinkish color. "My dad's a cop, remember? I know what's a crime and what ain't. But we ain't leaving 'til this car gets cleaned up. Now grab a rag and start scrubbing."

"No way. I am *not* helping you destroy evidence."

Kevin flung the rag at the bucket splashing pink water everywhere. His eyes narrowed to folded slits. "You know, I've had just about enough—"

The screen door creaked open and out stepped James. He looked like he hadn't gotten much sleep either. His hair stood out crazily in all directions like a peacock in a cyclone. He wet his lips uneasily. "I was hoping I was gonna wake up and Father Ted would be sitting here drinking coffee and having a cigarette and this would all have been a bad dream," he said.

Kevin said, "Dennis still asleep?"

"Yup. He's sure gonna be in for a surprise when he wakes up."

I cocked my eye in Kevin's direction. "This genius has taken it on himself to destroy evidence," I said.

Kevn shook his head. "Doofus here don't get it. The last thing we need is some cop pulling us over for some bullshit reason and finding blood all over the seats. Then we'll never get out here."

It just gets worse and worse, I thought. I went over and sat down on one of the milk crates, far enough away so that I had a good head start if Kevin decided to come after me. Then I spoke my piece. "You said we'd decide what we're gonna do this morning. But you seem to have already made up our minds for us."

Kevin leaned against the hood of the Jeep and folded his arms. "That's 'cause there's nothing to discuss. I've been going over it all morning while you slugs have been sleeping." He paused before he said the next thing. "I believe him."

"You believe who?" I said.

"Dennis, who do you think?" After a pause, he continued, "Look, I know the guy's no angel, but Father Ted must have done something to him, something real bad, like he said. Nothing else makes any sense." He took a breath. "Look at the facts." He held up his hand and began ticking off his fingers. "Number one, you got the pot and all the booze. Two, you got the dirty magazines. Three, he takes Dennis out on some backroad...Those are the facts, right? We can at least agree on that?"

Those might have been *some* of the facts. Another fact was that Dennis stabbed Father Ted thirty or forty times out there. Couldn't he have stabbed him once or twice and run away? Who the hell stabs someone forty times?

Besides Dennis's uncle, I mean.

I know, I wasn't there. And the rest of us had no clue what really happened. And we never would. I said, "Even if it was self-defense, there's still a dead priest lying out there in the woods...What happened to telling your dad?"

"We will. As soon as we get home. But we gotta get home first."

"Why not just call him now?"

"Do you see a phone out here?"

"So we drive into town! To a gas station!"

"I told you, Doofus, I know cops. I've been around them my whole life and I'm telling you we need to get the fuck out of Dodge." Kevin paused and took a breath. "Look, any minute now some hillbilly's gonna stumble on a dead priest out in the woods. And right after that the sheriff's gonna come looking for us. Then they're gonna find out who Dennis's uncle is and they're gonna drag our asses down to the basement of the jail and beat confessions out of us. And they ain't gonna stop 'til we say what they wanna hear, whether it's true or not."

I couldn't believe what I was hearing. I mean...is this what Kevin's dad did back in St. Louis? Beat false confessions out of innocent kids? Is that how he knew all this?

Or was he talking out of his ass like usual?

Kevin continued, "And the three of us...we ain't getting off that easy. At the very least they'll charge us as accessories. Accessories to murder." His eyes narrowed on me. "You wanna guess how many years you'll do for that?"

"You may be an accessory 'cause you destroyed evidence,

but I'm not!"

"You want to risk it? Or do you want to let my dad handle it when we get home?"

My chest tightened in anger, so tight I could hardly breath. "This is so fucked up!" I cried. Then I looked to James for moral support. "What do *you* say?" I asked him.

James's face was white as a Klansman's sheet. "I...I don't know."

I rubbed my face with my hands. "I don't believe this."

"There you go," Kevin said. "Three against one."

"He said he didn't know!"

Well *I* do," Kevin said. "It's simple. As soon as Dennis wakes up we're gonna pack up our shit and—"

"Not me!"

"Will you let me finish?"

I stormed off across the yard. Hell no, I wasn't going to let him finish. Everything was spinning completely out of control and there didn't seem to be a damn thing I could do to stop it. All I knew was that somehow I had to get away from these clowns before things got even worse.

Kevin's voice rose, drifting out over the yard. "We're gonna pack our shit up and get out of here. And as soon as we get home we can tell my dad what happened." He peered at me with little angry eyes. "We'll be home in three or four hours. You can wait three hours, can't you?"

I turned back to James. "You're not gonna go along with this?"

James gave a noncommittal shrug. "I like the idea of getting out of here. Goin' home."

"There you go," Kevin said. "I'm telling you, I know cops—"

"Yeah you've said that like five times," I said.

"Because it's true! I'm telling you, once they get their hands on us there's no telling what'll happen. We'll end up confessing to all kinds of shit. The Kennedy Assassination. *Both* of them.

Trust me, it happens all the time. And once you confess not even Perry Fucking Mason can get you off."

The screen door creaked open.

"Which one of you fuckers took a shit in my mouth and ran over my head with a garbage truck?" Dennis asked. He leaned unsteadily against the screen door and closed his eyes wincingly. He was shirtless and barefoot, wearing only some ratty jeans. He slowly sank to the concrete steps. He looked like he was in a lot of pain, like he *literally* had been run over by a garbage truck.

Kevin said, "We're packing up and getting the hell out of here right now. And when we get home we're gonna tell my dad what happened."

A long moment passed. Dennis stared at us blankly. "What do you mean, what happened?"

There was an astounded silence. Finally Kevin said, "You *do* remember what happened yesterday?"

Dennis hesitated. He clasped his legs with his arms and rested his chin on his knees. He sat there for a while, laboring to pull up yesterday's events. After a moment his face changed color and his eyes wavered like something faint and indistinct was coming back to him from a long distance. "Oh shit," he muttered.

"There's still some blood on the front seats if that'll help jog your memory," Kevin said.

Dennis stared at Kevin for a second, then he scraped his hands over his face. "I was hoping that was all a crazy dream."

"It was crazy...but no dream," Kevin said.

We stood there silently, for a long time, watching Dennis. His face paled and I saw sudden terror on it. He said, "We can't say nothing about this to no one...ever."

Kevin said, "We've already had that discussion. Yesterday. Only you were too fucking drunk to remember."

Dennis locked eyes with Kevin.

"Anyway it's already been decided," Kevin said. "When we

get home we're gonna tell my dad what happened. He's a cop."

I said, "You mean *you've* decided!"

Kevin glared at me, then he turned back to Dennis. "My dad will believe you," he said.

"Your dad?" Dennis cried. "He don't matter! It's the cops down here…the prosecutor…they're the only ones that matter!" Dennis took a long breath. "Your dad! Lotta fucking good that'll do."

I stood numbly, unable to believe it. Not only did Dennis refuse to go to the sheriff, which was the obvious thing to do, he didn't even want to tell Kevin's dad. The psycho didn't want to tell anyone.

"Well, we gotta tell someone!" Kevin said.

"No. We don't!" Dennis said. "Don't you get it? He was a fucking priest! I'm just some…I'm just some juvenile delinquent whose uncle's sittin' on death row."

Kevin tossed aside the rag he'd been holding. It landed in a puddle of water and lay there in a grayish pink lump of despair. "Fuck that!" Kevin snapped. "It's already been decided! We're gonna let my dad straighten it out."

"Your dad can't do shit!" Dennis cried. "He's nothing but a two-bit dirty cop! Nobody down here gives a damn what he says!"

A darkness filled Kevin's eyes as he fought to keep his cool. "Yeah? So what do you suggest we do?"

A moment ticked by.

Dennis suddenly went grave. "Bury him."

Kevin shook his head slightly. "Yeah, you said that yesterday. And how do we explain his disappearance? Say he drowned in the river or got eaten by a bear?"

Dennis hesitated. You could almost hear the synapses misfiring as his booze-and-nicotine-soaked brain struggled to put together more than two thoughts. "Then we go home and say he dropped us off at the rectory and that was the last we saw of him."

"For the last goddamn time," I cried, "we ain't burying nobody!"

I don't think they even heard me. It was like I wasn't even there.

Kevin put his eyes on Dennis, flat and hard. "Do you even know what you're asking? You want us to help you cover up..." His voice trailed off. His eyes narrowed and he shook his head. "I mean, I wouldn't even do that for my own brother, why the hell would I do it for you?"

"You said you believed me! All of you did. Well do ya or don't ya?"

Nobody answered.

"Godammit, do you believe me or not?"

We glanced around uneasily. Finally Kevin cleared his throat and said, "I...I think what you did was self-defense. And that ain't a crime. But you're acting like you committed a terrible...like you *murdered* someone." He paused and glanced back at me and James. "Look, we're willing to meet you halfway. Let's get the hell out of here and when we get home we'll tell my dad what happened and—"

Dennis hopped to his feet. "That ain't halfway! That's as good as turning me over to the sheriff. The St. Louis cops will just arrest my ass and they'll drag me right back here." He took a breath. "I'll tell you something else. If *I* go to jail, *we all* go to jail!"

Was that a threat? Was he threatening us? Was the son of a bitch going to say we helped him kill Father Ted if we didn't go along with him?

Kevin sighed again and looked off for a moment. "Why'd you have to do it? Why couldn't you have just punched him in the nuts and run off?"

"I tried," Dennis said through his teeth. "Don't you think I tried? I tell you I didn't have a choice." He stared off, thinking. "I don't even remember knifing him. But I must have."

"Yeah, like forty times," Kevin said.

I sat down on a broken milk crate. I felt like a grenade had gone off inside me. Like my insides were completely hollowed out. It seemed like whatever we ended up doing, it would be decided by Kevin and Dennis. Two half-wits. Even together they still came up short of a whole. James and I were mere spectators, with no say in what could turn out to be the most important decision of our lives.

We seemed to have reached an impasse. Nothing was said for a few minutes. Then, out of a long silence, James said, "Let's bury the child-molesting son of a bitch."

I stood stunned for a minute, unable to believe what I was hearing. I don't think Kevin believed it either.

"What?" he finally managed to say.

James's hands curled into fists, then straightened. "Bury him," he said.

For a moment I wondered if Father Ted hadn't done something to him too. I mean, why else would he go along with Dennis?

We all turned to look at Kevin. His face looked as blank and inscrutable as ever.

It was now two against two.

And then it wasn't. I swear Kevin changed his mind just so he wouldn't be on the same side as me. No other reason.

"What the hell," he said resignedly. "My dad probably couldn't have done anything anyway—even if he wanted to. He ain't even a sergeant."

"Wait a minute!" I cried, bounding to my feet. "You're not serious?"

"It's decided," Kevin said. "Three against one." He stepped toward me and jabbed his finger in my chest, knocking me back a step. "You're outvoted, Doofus." He turned to look at James and Dennis. "Ain't that right, fellas?"

"Fuckin' A," Dennis said.

Kevin peered at James for a moment. "Right, James?"

He couldn't even look at me. He just studied the air to the

left of him. Finally, he wiped at his nose and grunted, "Uh-huh."

And just like that, the matter was settled.

"WE'RE GONNA NEED a better plan," Kevin said.

That much was obvious. Dennis's plan wasn't a real plan. It wasn't even the concept of a plan. It didn't account for Father Ted's sudden disappearance or a hundred other eventualities that might come up.

Not to worry, though. We could always count on Kevin to take charge. He sat down next to Dennis and said, "So your idea is we bury him out by some cornfield and drive home and say he dropped us off at the rectory and we never saw him again?"

Dennis nodded. "Kiss," he said.

"What?" Kevin said icily.

"K-I-S-S. Keep it simple, stupid," Dennis said.

"Stupid is right," Kevin said. "What happens after that?"

"What do you mean?"

"We're supposed to drive up to the rectory and leave the Jeep and then what? Hope nobody notices that Father Ted isn't with us? What about Monsignor or the housekeeper or the janitor?"

"It'll be Saturday," Dennis said. "No janitor. And it's the housekeeper's day off."

I wondered how he knew that. Then I got a bad feeling about how he knew that.

Kevin shook his head. "That ain't gonna work."

"You got a better idea?"

Kevin nodded his head slowly. "First of all, we don't go back to the rectory. I drop you off a block or two from your houses. Then I ditch the Jeep somewhere, down by the river, make it look like Father Ted got into some kind of trouble. We leave some booze and some of that pot in the Jeep."

JACKS FORK

Right away I noticed several holes in Kevin's brilliant plan. "Why would he still be driving the Jeep instead of his own car?" I said.

"Could be a lotta reasons," Kevin said.

"Name one."

I waited.

Kevin looked straight ahead, his jaw as rigid as a lead pipe. "Look, it's good enough for now. And it's a hell of a lot better than *his* plan." He scratched his cheek. "Now let's find some shovels."

"Seriously?" I said. "*Good enough?*"

Once again, no one paid any attention to me. Instead they went around to the back of the house where an old rusted shed leaned in the weeds. But any shovels that had been inside had been stolen years ago.

"We're gonna have to drive to the hardware store," Kevin said. "What's a pair of shovels cost?"

Dennis casually drew a billfold from his back pocket and opened it revealing a thick wad of bills. "Got us covered," he said.

Something about all those bills didn't sit right with me. I said, "Where'd you get all that cash?"

"Father Ted. He won't be needing it."

My jaw dropped. "You *stole* his wallet?"

"I didn't steal it. You can't steal from a dead person."

"You *stole* his fucking wallet!"

"Don't be a putz," Dennis said. "If someone does find him and he ain't got a wallet he'll be harder to identify."

"Were you gonna tell us about this," Kevin said in a sudden belligerent voice, "or just keep it to yourself?"

Dennis smirked and thumbed through the bills. "I just told you, didn't I?" His eyes darted over our faces. "*R*elax, It's gas money. And shovel money now. Maybe we'll get a bite to eat on the way home."

"Unbelievable," I said.

"How much is in there?" Kevin said.

"I ain't counted it. Not much."

"Well, count it!"

Dennis bristled at being told what to do, but he grudgingly counted the money. Twice he messed up and had to start over. "Ninety-one bucks, give or take," he said.

"That's a lot of shovels and gas," Kevin said.

Dennis didn't say anything to that. He slipped the wallet back into his pocket and drew a cigarette from behind his ear. The guy literally had smokes stashed everywhere.

For a brief moment Kevin looked like he might be reconsidering things, like maybe this latest stunt was the last straw. Then he let out a long breath and said, "Let's go get them shovels." He turned and leveled his gaze at me. "Are we all on the same page here?"

I studied the three of them, their faces etched with fear and ignorance and contempt. How could I ever think of going along with these guys?

Then again, what choice did I have? I might very well end up like Father Ted if I didn't.

So, yeah, I'd go along. At least for now.

"Yeah," I said.

"Yeah what?"

"Yeah, we're on the same stupid page."

I eased into the back seat. James got in on the other side and Kevin slid behind the wheel. Dennis told us to hang on while he went inside to get something. A moment later he came out waving a pint of Wild Turkey. "Hair of the dog," he said and eased into the front passenger side. He cracked the seal on the bottle and took a long swallow, then he offered the bottle around. This time there were no takers. He shrugged and said, "More for me."

Kevin cranked the engine. "I don't care how much you drink, your ass is digging that hole."

Dennis picked up Father Ted's Panama hat from the dashboard and crammed it down over his eyes and leaned his head back on the headrest. *"Dig a hole, dig a hole in the meadow,"* he sang. *"Dig a hole in the cold, cold ground!"*

"You're one creepy-ass motherfucker," Kevin said.

Dennis laughed and gave us all his big old goofy grin.

CHAPTER 7

WE FOUND AN open True Value Hardware Store on Main Street and we bought a spade and a round point and some bleach and baking soda and a couple of sponges.

"Why not buy some crime-scene tape, too, while we're at it?" I muttered as we made our way to the checkout counter.

"Shut the fuck up," Kevin said.

Fortunately for us, the bored, homely, teenage girl behind the cash register didn't seem to notice or care what we were purchasing. She was interested only in Dennis, who was still running around barefoot and bare-chested—despite the NO SHOES, NO SHIRT, NO SERVICE sign on the entrance—and smoking a cigarette—despite the no-smoking signs—and toting a pint of whiskey in the back pocket of his jeans. She must have had a thing for bad boys.

We paid for the tools and stuff with Father Ted's cash and piled back into the Jeep and drove toward the outskirts of town. We passed a little roadside produce stand and stopped and bought a sack of Jonathan apples from an old farm couple. They were real small-town friendly and could've talked to us for hours. Of course, they didn't know we were dangerous city kids on our way to dispose of the body of a priest that one of us had stabbed to death.

It was going on one o'clock and our fine summer-blue morning sky had gone overcast and gray and the temperature had dipped a good ten degrees. We found our turn-off easily in the daylight and once again my stomach muscles knotted as we slowly rumbled across the rickety old truss bridge. It didn't look like anyone had been down the tractor lane since we'd left. No fresh tracks, anyway. We drove till we spied some large, basketball-sized bloodstains in the dust which we hadn't noticed in the dark. We parked and Kevin got out and kicked dust over the bloodstains. James strode around to the back of the Jeep and picked up one of the shovels and Kevin grabbed the other.

"Give it to him," Kevin told James and he fixed me with two evil brown eyes.

"I don't mind digging for a while," James said.

"I said give it to *him*. I want *him* to dig."

I knew what he was doing. He wanted me to help with the burying so they'd have that hanging over me too. It was stupid; if it came down to that, I could just say they forced me to dig. Which was the sort of the truth.

James hesitated a moment. Like me and Dennis, he may have been afraid of Kevin, but he also did not like being told what to do. He grudgingly handed me the shovel.

Dennis was leaning on the door of the Jeep dragging on a smoke, Father Ted's Panama hat resting on the back of his head, the car stereo on. The same awful cassette tape played low.

E-lec-tri-cal banana…gonna be a sud-den craze…

"Turn that shit off," Kevin shouted. "You want someone to hear us?"

"Quite rightly," Dennis said. Then he reached through the open window and snapped off the stereo.

Kevin glanced at James. "All we need is for your cousin to drain the battery and get us stuck out here with a dead corpse on our hands."

James pulled down the tailgate and took a seat. He shrugged and didn't say a word.

Kevin and I headed for the thicket. When we got within view of Father Ted's body, Kevin halted suddenly. I thought he must have gotten a noseful of rotten-corpse smell, but that wasn't it. It was too soon for that. Kevin shook his head dismally. "Oh man, some animals got to him last night."

I kept my eyes on my shoes. No way was I looking at that.

Kevin turned away and studied the nearby woods for a moment, looking for God knows what. Then he motioned with his head toward a nearby gully. "There. We'll dig down there."

I followed Kevin up a small rise and down the gully, using the shovel for balance. The gully was mostly dry and full of dangling roots and last fall's leaves and branches and some small fallen trees.

"Here," Kevin said.

A gully seemed like a dumb place to bury a body. Had he never heard of erosion? Wouldn't stormwater wash away the soil? I didn't say anything, though. I figured it didn't matter since I was going to tell my parents what happened when we got home and he'd be dug up in a week anyway.

Probably.

I set to work with the spade biting into the heavy clay soil. The work was exhausting and maddeningly slow. After five minutes of hard digging I had the depressing realization that my mom and dad still thought I was on a fun camping trip…floating on a lazy river with good friends.

I could feel Kevin's eyes on me. I waited for him to comment on my digging technique.

It wasn't a long wait.

"Jesus, Doofus, who taught you to use a shovel?"

Right on cue. I was *so* close to clobbering him with my spade. Maybe I'd bury two bodies at once. I said, "If you don't like how I do it, do it yourself."

That shut him up for a little while.

After thirty minutes of digging I was dead tired and my hands were raw and bleeding. A couple of nice fat blisters had popped up on my palms and fingers. Of course we hadn't thought to buy work gloves.

I noticed how Dennis and James were taking it easy, lolling against the trunk of a fallen tree and helping themselves to the sack of Jonathans. Dennis snickered at something James said and drew a jackknife from his back pocket and cut a wedge out of the apple. He popped the slice between his lips and chewed with his mouth open.

Kevin was watching this too. His eyes were wide with disbelief, then he stabbed his shovel into the dirt. "Are you fucking kidding me? You've still got that knife?"

Dennis brough another slice of apple to his mouth. "What about it?" he said between bites. "I cleaned it."

"Are you insane? If the cops find that on you you're fucked. We're all fucked. You gotta get rid of that thing now!"

Dennis studied the knife. "This knife cost me ten bucks. It's a good knife. Lotta good memories. I think I'll hang onto it."

Kevin's eyes flashed and his voice turned husky with rage. "Seriously? You're gonna risk going to jail over a ten-dollar knife?"

"I done told you, I'm keeping the knife."

Kevin clambered out of the gully. He didn't even glance at Dennis and James in passing. "That's it. I'm done 'til he gets rid of that knife," he said. He went over to the Jeep and got into the driver's seat and sat there stewing silently.

I climbed out of the gully and sat down on the ground with my legs drawn up to my chest and got ready for another long delay.

Dennis took another bite of apple and chewed it thoughtfully. He held the knife out in front of him and admired it, turning it this way and that, trying to catch a glint of sun. Then he slowly got to his feet. I wasn't sure what he was going to do with the knife. A guy like him might do anything. Suddenly he reared back and tossed the knife as far as he could. He had a good strong arm. The knife sailed about fifty yards in a long high arc and was swallowed up by the woods.

Dennis's eyes narrowed to slits as he turned and glared at Kevin. "Happy?"

Kevin chewed at a thumbnail. Then he slowly eased out of the Jeep. "I'd have been happier if you'd thrown it in a pond...or buried it."

"Yeah, well we can't have everything." Dennis popped the last slice of apple into his mouth and tossed away the core.

Kevin and I went back to digging. We worked on the hole for another five minutes before I figured I'd done my share. I studied our progress. The hole was about six feet long by three feet wide. Maybe two feet deep. I climbed up out of the gully. I was weary, sweaty, filthy and thirsty as hell, but there was no water. We'd forgotten that too. I went over to where Dennis sat and dropped the spade at his feet. He studied the shovel for a second, looked at me, then he turned and drew another apple from the sack and bit into it with a loud wet crunch. He didn't say a word, he just stared at me and slowly chewed his apple.

James, meanwhile, went to relieve Kevin, who climbed wearily out of the gully and trudged back to the Jeep. He opened the driver's-side door and slid in behind the wheel. He rested his arms across the wheel and lay his head on his arms. From where I stood, it looked like he was crying. But I knew better than that.

I turned back to Dennis. I could feel anger swelling in my throat. "When are you gonna get off your ass and do something?"

Dennis tossed away the half-eaten apple and took off Father Ted's hat and set it down on the log. Then he got to his feet in stages and picked up the shovel. He glanced at me briefly with a blank look on his face, then he tramped up the slope, dragging the shovel behind him.

I felt a sudden and desperate need to be by myself, so I tramped off through the woods, drifting where the going was easy and the foliage not so dense, until I came to the bend in the creek. As soon as I sat down on the bank all the fear and rage and hopelessness I'd been holding inside came loose and shook me like a fever and the back of my throat started to burn like I'd swallowed battery acid. *You got to keep it together, man*, I thought. *This ain't no time to fall apart or sit around feeling sorry for yourself. Your pity party is going to have to wait until you get home.*

So I got to my feet and started back. Coming out of the thicket I saw a blue Dodge pickup shamble down the county road and turn in at the entrance to the tractor lane. The truck came to a stop a few yards from the highway and sat idling loudly for a moment. Southern rock spilled out the open windows. I held my breath and stood motionless by the side of the road. Dennis and James leaned on their shovels and waited.

A minute or two passed and nothing happened. I was beginning to work out an escape plan in my head when the truck backed up, turned, and went back down the highway the way it had come.

Kevin leaned out of the Jeep and shouted, "Hurry it the fuck up!"

Seconds later, Dennis tossed his shovel onto the three-foot mound of dirt ringing the grave and stepped out. He shook a smoke out of a crumpled Lucky Strike pack. James followed him up out of the hole.

"Good enough," Dennis said.

Kevin eased out of the truck and walked over and stood at the edge of the gully and inspected the hole. I figured he'd have something critical to say, but all he said was, "Do you think that dude in the pickup saw us?"

Dennis lighted his smoke. "If we could see him, he could see us."

James said, "He could be on the phone right now to the owner of this property."

It got quiet for a moment as we all thought about that.

"You're being paranoid," Kevin said. But he looked scared.

And worried.

James took off his big clunky glasses and rubbed the lenses on his polo shirt. "Well...what are we waiting for?"

"I don't know about you," Dennis said, "but I'm gonna have a snort." He drew the pint of Wild Turkey from his back pocket and took a long pull off the bottle.

"Let's go get him," Kevin said to me and James.

I nodded toward Dennis. "Isn't that psycho gonna help?"

"Let's just finish this," Kevin said.

That seemed to settle it.

This time I got a good accidental look at Father Ted. Whatever had gotten to him during the night had chewed off bits and pieces of his nose and ears. James must have gotten a good look too, because he immediately stooped over and vomited. And that set off a chain reaction. Soon I was down on all fours dry-heaving my guts up. Kevin leaned against a scrub oak and waited for us to finish.

It was a long wait.

Finally he lifted his eyebrows at us. "If you're done, cover that shit up. We're not leaving any clues behind."

James got to his feet and kicked some dirt and leaves over the vomit, and then the three of us went over and stood around the remains of Father Ted.

"Ready?" Kevin said.

James swallowed nervously and nodded. Kevin got Father Ted up under the armpits and James and I each took a leg and we hefted him, dragging him about six inches off the ground. When we reached the gully we stopped and set him down. We had a choice to make. We could either carry him down into the gully somehow and drag him over to the grave or we could swing him from the edge of the gully and hope he landed in the hole. The first way would be the most dignified. The second way would be the quickest and easiest.

The three of us stood and looked at each other.

"On the count of three," Kevin said.

It was settled then. I took hold of Father Ted's right ankle and James took hold of the left one and we swung him, one, two, three times, then we let go.

He landed with a loud thud. He missed the grave by a good three feet.

Kevin hopped down into the gully and rolled Father Ted into the hole, then he climbed back up out of the gully, wiping his hands on his jeans.

For a moment we stood at the rim of the gully, staring down into the grave. James cleared his throat and said, "Should we say something? A prayer or something."

"Are you fucking kidding me?" Kevin said.

Those were my thoughts exactly. I picked up the spade and we strode back to the little clearing where we'd left Dennis.

"Cover him up," Kevin told Dennis. "And when you're done put some leaves and limbs over it." He glanced at the Panama hat sitting atop the log. "And don't forget that fucking hat." Kevin didn't wait for a response, he just walked down to the Jeep and eased into the driver's seat. He sat there with his resting on the wheel and his chin on his arm and his eyes staring blankly down the tractor lane. I swear he looked like he'd aged ten years. I guess we all did.

I went around to the rear of the Jeep and tossed the spade into the back. I thought about getting into the passenger side, but I decided not to. It seemed like the two guys most responsible for what happened should sit up front. I got in the back seat and James eased in beside me and we sat there for a while, dead tired and all puked out. Nobody felt like saying anything.

We waited for Dennis to move his ass, to go finish the job so we could get the hell out of there.

For a long time Dennis just sat there. I don't know what his deal was. Maybe he didn't like being told what to do. Five minutes passed. It seemed a lot longer. Kevin's face turned hard. He was about ready to hop out of the Jeep and beat the shit out of him when Dennis got up and stomped off into the woods.

Kevin let go a heavy sigh and turned on the radio and that goddamn song "Mellow Yellow" came on again. He punched the eject button and pulled the cassette out and threw it on the floorboards and stomped on it until it lay in a dozen pieces.

"Thank you," I said.

CHAPTER 8

BACK AT THE RANCH HOUSE I took a cold shower and changed into a clean T-shirt. I rolled up my sleeping bag and crammed my dirty clothes into my duffel and carried everything out to the Jeep. Then I went off by myself so I could think.

Try to think, anyway.

We were getting more and more freaked out by Dennis's behavior. He was hitting the bottle hard and acting crazier than a shithouse rat. I mean, I got it. I was barely holding it together myself. The only way I could keep my sanity was by constantly reminding myself that in a few hours I'd be back home, safe and secure in my bedroom.

Thank God that Kevin had made Dennis get rid of his knife. I didn't think Dennis would try anything after I "agreed" to go along with their stupid plan—but you never knew. I was still the one most likely to turn him in, the one least on board with their idiotic scheme. Dennis must have thought plenty about what I'd do once we got back to the city and we went our separate ways.

"Hey." James strode around the side of the house lugging the muddy shovels.

"We ready to go?" I said.

"Dennis is still in the shower."

"Still? He's been in there like fifteen minutes."

"Takes a long time to get the smell of death off you."

"He'll never get it off," I said. "None of us will."

"Don't be a drama queen," James said. "Anyway, my conscience is clear." He went over to the shed. A minute later, he came back without the shovels. I scooted over to give him room and he sat down beside me on the cinder block steps and let out a heavy sigh.

I said, "Ain't you gonna hide them better than that?"

"It ain't the shovels I'm worried about them finding."

I grunted.

James studied me carefully for a long time. "Did you mean it when you said you weren't gonna tell?"

I breathed in steadily and looked around. I tried to imagine telling someone—my mom and dad, for instance—that Father Ted had tried to rape Dennis Hailey so Dennis stabbed him to death.

They'd never believe it. Not in a million years.

That's what I told James. That my folks would never believe it.

James nodded. "Yeah, mine wouldn't either. Priests are chosen by God. That's what my mother says. Handpicked by Christ."

"He ought to find someone else to do his picking for him."

I suppose I could tell my brother or my sister, I thought. Though I wasn't sure what they could do, or if they'd believe me either. I didn't have the reputation of a pathological liar, nor was I the most truthful kid in the world. I was somewhere in between.

I gazed out over the backyard where sage grass and bull thistle ran wild back to an old post-and-rail fence. Beyond the fence a dilapidated red barn with a roof advertisement for Meramec Caverns (SEE JESSE JAMES HIDEOUT) leaned precariously among the sad remnants of a pecan orchard. Everything looked wild and abandoned. Like old Jesse James would have liked it.

"What's Kevin doing?" I said.

"Sitting in the Jeep, drooling over them magazines."

"Jesus, how can he look at naked girls at a time like this?"

"I can look at naked girls any time."

He had a point, I guess.

We were silent. I studied a pair of doves balancing on a nearby telephone line while James swatted at a stubbornly persistent horsefly. I still hadn't been able to get a good read on him—why all the sudden he'd decided to go along with Dennis. If he truly believed Dennis, or if he was just going along because they were cousins. Or because of peer pressure.

There was only one way to find out. "So you don't have any doubts about Dennis's story?"

James shrugged. "Why would he make up something like that? Guys don't make up getting raped by guys. Maybe by a woman, but not by a guy."

"He stole Father Ted's wallet."

"He didn't kill Father Ted for ninety bucks."

"I don't know. I guess I'm not as sure as you are." I wiped the sweat out of my eyes and we grew moody and silent again. Despite the overcast skies, the day was—as they say—hot as Satan's buttcrack. The pesky horsefly returned for seconds and this time I flattened him with the palm of my hand.

James said, "You're thinking about Dennis's uncle."

"Aren't you? What did *he* kill for? A pack of cigarettes, a bottle of cheap wine?"

James didn't respond. He toed at something buried in a clump of weeds. An old empty shotgun shell. Red with a gold cap. There were probably thousands of them around here.

There was something I'd been meaning to ask James for a while and this seemed as good a time as any. "You said Father Ted never tried anything with you."

"Yeah, so?"

"Nothing even a little weird?"

"Nothing," he said peevishly. Then he must have had second

thoughts. "Actually...well, there *was* this one time." He paused, like he was debating whether he should go on. "Once during school he did take me and Paul Hendricks up to his room. I guess we were in eighth grade. Seventh or eighth. I don't remember why he got us out of class. He said he had to go up to his room to get something so we went with him. I didn't think nothing of it. I thought it might be cool to see a priest's room." He cut his eyes at me and continued. "So we get up to his room and the bottom drawers of his dresser are wide open and you can see all these dirty magazines sitting out plain as day. I remember thinking, why are they just out in the open like that? Isn't he afraid the housekeeper will see them? Or the monsignor?"

I stared at James, my eyes widening. "And then what happened?"

"Nothing. We went back to class."

A moment passed and I said, "So you knew there was something a little creepy about him?"

"I guess so...but I never said anything about it. I never mentioned it. Until now, anyway."

"Why not?"

James shrugged his shoulders. "I guess I didn't want to get him in trouble. Everybody liked him, ya know? He wasn't a dick like most priests...like your uncle. Everyone thought he was cool...So he liked looking at pictures of naked women? Who doesn't? It's not a sin, is it?"

I wasn't sure. I suspect our teachers, all School Sisters of Notre Dame, would have said, *Hell yes, it's a sin. The sin of lust. One of the Seven Deadly Sins.* My mother certainly would have said that.

But then you think about all those paintings, those religious works of art with naked women in them, chicks with their boobs hanging out. That's not a sin.

Wasn't it supposed to be what was in your heart that made it a sin?

We went silent for a while, thinking our thoughts. I could see not wanting to get Father Ted in trouble; he'd been more like a friend than an associate pastor. You don't rat out your friends because they have stacks of *Beaver Hunt* magazine under their mattresses. It was nobody's business.

If only it had been that innocent. That simple.

I said, "So even though you knew he was a porn addict you still came on this trip?"

James gave me his shrug again. "How often do I get to go on a float trip?"

I nodded knowingly.

"This is my first time," he said. He looked impassively into the distance. "Does your dad keep any of that...*Playboys* and shit?"

"My dad? Hell no."

"Why not?"

"I don't know. He just doesn't...Does yours?"

"My mother would never allow that, even if he wanted to."

"Same here."

We sat for a while thinking about things, then I said, "Would your dad ever give booze to fifteen-year-olds?"

"He doesn't even like giving me a sip of his beer."

But Father Ted did. And look where he took Dennis, way the hell out in the middle of a cornfield. What more did I need to know?

I remembered his creepy remark about strip poker, too.

Maybe I could understand why James had changed his tune so suddenly.

Okay, so there was definitely something profoundly off about Father Ted, but Dennis was a certifiable nutcase, too. Even if I half-believed Dennis, I did not agree with any of the rest of it: the lies, the cover-up, the destruction of evidence. Nor did I think the police would simply dismiss our story as a pack of lies told by a bloodthirsty teenage priest-killing gang.

Or maybe they would, once they figured out who Dennis's

uncle was. Once they got a look at the thirty or forty knife wounds. Once they found out that we'd buried his corpse in a shallow grave by a cornfield.

James said, "So what do you think of Kevin's plan?"

I made sure the others weren't within earshot. "Here's what I don't get—why we're letting the dumbest and craziest guys we know make the plans."

James frowned at me. "I don't think it's half bad."

"Half bad? You're gonna settle for half bad?"

"I said I *don't* think it's half bad."

"Then how bad is it?"

A loud voice startled us. "Let's hit the road!"

Kevin.

I got to my feet. "Maybe we're finally getting out of here."

"But you're not gonna tell, right?"

I didn't answer. I was too angry to answer. I strode around to the front of the house where Dennis was tossing bags into the back of the Jeep. At least two of them, I noticed, had belonged to Father Ted. The ones stuffed with liquor and girlie magazines.

I walked up behind him. "What are you doing?"

Dennis slammed the tailgate. "Did you forget? We gotta leave some of that grass and booze in the Jeep when we ditch it."

"Maybe not the grass," Kevin said. "If a state trooper pulls us over and he finds that he'll lock us up sure as shit."

"You worry too much."

"I'm worrying for the both of us."

After the Jeep was loaded up, Kevin whistled loudly to get our attention. James and I gathered around. Dennis sat in the open door of the Jeep.

"Before we go, we need to get our stories straight in case somebody comes around asking about Father Ted."

"What do you mean 'in case?'" I said. "Everyone's favorite priest is missing and we're gonna be the last ones that saw him.

Of course they're gonna ask us."

Kevin gave me a dark look. "That's why we need to have our stories straight, Doofus." Then he turned a serious face to Dennis, who was studying the ruined Donovan cassette tape and looking like his dog had just died.

"Goddamn it, Dennis, are you listening?"

Dennis hurled the cassette across the yard and sank dejectedly back into his seat. He took Father Ted's Panama hat from the dash and pulled it down over his eyes. I got the feeling that Dennis didn't care what happened anymore. Whether we went to prison or we got away with it, it was all the same to him. Maybe the cold, grim realization of what he'd done had finally sunk in. Maybe he realized that no matter what happened things would never be the same, that they were going to be worse, much worse, and he couldn't imagine how things could possibly be worse than they had been, so he'd said to hell with it and he'd given up.

Who could blame him?

Kevin's face tightened for a moment, then he said, "We need to account for what we've been doing...ever since it happened. Last night and today." He thought for a moment. "Like today, we were supposed to go canoeing again. But there'd probably be a record of who rented canoes. You see what I'm saying?"

"So what'll we do?" James asked.

"We could say we went hiking."

"Where'd we go hiking?" I said.

"You know that trail we passed on the way in? I think it was called Spring Branch Trail?"

"I don't remember that," James said. "I remember passing one called Welch Springs Trail."

Kevin looked at me hopefully. I said I didn't remember passing either one, which was true. I'd been lying in the cargo compartment staring up at an evil cloud of cigarette smoke hovering just above my nose.

Kevin turned to look at Dennis. "What about you?"

Dennis was rooting through one of Father Ted's duffel bags. "Where'd that bag of grass go? There was a whole bag in here."

"I threw it out," Kevin said.

"You what?" Dennis's eyes took on that wild, disturbed quality again. "Are you nuts?"

"Yeah, I'm nuts." He turned back to James: "You're sure about that? Welch Spring Trail?"

James thought it over for a moment. "Pretty sure."

"The whole bag?" Dennis cried.

"Yes! The whole bag!" Kevin threw his hands up and his face went dark with exasperation. When he turned back to me and James he said, "So, instead of going canoeing we went hiking. On Welch Springs Trail. Remember. Welch. Like the jelly."

"Jelly," James said.

"Let's say we got back here 'round five o'clock and Father Ted said we'd better leave tonight instead of tomorrow—"

"Because?" I said.

"Because one of us got sick."

James and I shared a pair of raised eyebrows.

Kevin's gaze shifted to James. "You had heat exhaustion. Vomiting. A headache."

"Why me?" James said.

"Where?" Dennis said angrily. "Where'd you get rid of it?"

"Will you shut up about that!" Kevin snapped.

Dennis flung the duffel bag onto the floorboards, muttering swear words under his breath.

After Dennis quieted down, I said, "Wouldn't he have called our parents if we were coming home early? Especially if one of us was sick?"

Kevin thought about that. "He tried to, but nobody was home."

That seems unlikely, I thought.

James said, "What about last night?"

Kevin thought for a moment. "Last night we ate the rest of

the food and then we played cards and then we went to bed…We played seven-card stud with bloody knuckles."

I shuffled my feet nervously waiting for more. "That's it?" I said.

"And the last time we saw Father Ted was when he dropped us off at our houses," Kevin said. "And listen up, because this is crucial. He didn't say a word about what he was gonna do after that. We have no clue what he did after he dropped us off."

Kevin studied Dennis for a moment. He was slouched in the passenger seat, one of Father Ted's cigarettes tilted from his lips. "Did you get that, Dennis?"

He was obviously still pissed about the pot. He hit the cigarette and sent a jet of smoke out the open door. "Wasn't yours to get rid of," he muttered.

Kevin cursed at the top of his lungs: "Jesus Christ man, what *is* your fucking deal? We're doing this for you! We could all go to jail for this and all you care about is a stupid bag of dope!"

Dennis removed the butt from his lips and snapped it across the yard. "You oughta be thanking me. I'm the one that rid society of that evil fucker."

Kevin threw up his hands. "That's it. I'm done."

For the first time ever Kevin looked defeated. Like things had gotten to be too much for him. He turned and trudged back to the house.

Worser and worser, I thought.

It looked like our departure was being delayed again. I began wandering around the yard aimlessly, trying to work out some nervous energy. There were holes the size of a school bus in Kevin's story. Like why Father Ted wouldn't have dropped us at our houses (instead of a block away) and why, after he dropped us off, he would have kept driving around in the Franklin's Jeep and not his Mustang. There were probably a lot more holes that I couldn't see, but that the cops might.

A few minutes later, Kevin was back outside. He glanced at his watch and said, "Let's get out here."

I went around the Jeep and eased into the backseat next to my old buddy James. Kevin got in behind the wheel. He turned slightly to address the three of us.

"Just try to keep our stories straight. And as for what really happened down here—we never talk about it again. Not to anybody. Not to your family, not to your friends, and sure as hell not to a priest." He studied us. "Are we square on that?"

I turned to look at James. He stared blankly out his window. "Uh-huh," he said.

"Roy?"

The bastard was calling me Roy because he knew I wouldn't respond otherwise.

"Uh-huh," I said. Then I turned and looked out my window.

Of course I didn't mean it. I would have said anything to get out of there.

CHAPTER 9

THE SIGN SAID there was a Shell gas station a half mile from the Highway 72 exit. We hated the idea of stopping so soon, but we had no choice. We were literally driving on fumes. The patrol car was hiding in the parking lot of the little United Pentecostal Church we drove past. That was not cool at all, hiding behind a church. But I guess there weren't any walls separating church and state in Iron County. Kevin had been cautiously observing the forty-five-mile-per-hour speed limit, but once we left the highway there were no speed limit signs. Or maybe the patrolman got a good look at four underage boys in a Jeep and thought: *Why that there looks like a code 11-54, a suspicious veehicle.*

The patrol car zipped right up on our bumper, lights flashing. Kevin let loose a long string of expletives and pounded on the steering wheel. The siren bleeped jarringly. The sound sent shock waves all the way down to my anal sphincter.

James shook his head wretchedly. "We were *so* close to getting away with it."

"He sees all the children of men," Dennis muttered.

"I couldn't have been doing more than thirty!" Kevin cried.

"What's the speed limit?" James said.

"How the hell do I know? There aren't any signs. Probably whatever that redneck pig says it is."

Kevin sat up straight and tall behind the wheel. He narrowed his eyes at Dennis who had somehow chanced upon another pint of whiskey. "Put that bottle under the seat!" he snapped. "And roll down the windows. It smells like a distillery in here!"

Dennis didn't utter a word of protest as he rolled down his window. Kevin drew over to the shoulder of the road and we all nervously studied the cruiser in the side mirrors. The worst of it was that I could see the yellow Shell sign just beyond the next hill. That's how close we'd gotten.

Kevin turned his head and gave me and James a hard stare. "I'll do the talking," he said. Then he looked at Dennis. "And not a word out of you."

"I got nothing to say to the pig, except oink, fucking oink," Dennis said.

"You do and it'll be the last thing you ever say," Kevin said.

A thousand thoughts crashed through my mind at once. Foremost among them was the fear that they had found Father Ted and we were all about to be picked up for his murder. Someone—maybe whoever was in the blue Dodge pickup—had seen us out on the tractor lane and called the landowner who had taken his bloodhound out there and poked around and the hound had quickly sniffed out the shallow grave.

That's what my paranoid mind was telling me, anyway.

The deputy was taking his own sweet time. He was toying with us. Making us sweat. This was probably the highlight of his day and he was milking it for all it was worth.

Then a thought occurred to me: here was my chance! I could say something to this deputy. When he got up to the Jeep I could stick my head out the window and blurt out: *"It was Dennis killed him! And they forced me to go along, against my will!"* And Dennis and Kevin couldn't touch me. I could jump out of the car and put the deputy between me and them. Who knows, I might even catch a break for snitching on them, for being the first to squeal.

Only...

JACKS FORK

Only I knew I couldn't do it. No matter how much I hated those guys, I couldn't rat them out like that. Especially not on the spur of the moment. It wasn't that I was scared of them. (Well, maybe a little.) I truly don't know what it was. Some kind of primal tribe loyalty? Maybe it was the Missouri version of Stockholm Syndrome. Anyway, they hadn't made me do shit. I mean, sure, there was peer pressure, but they hadn't put a gun to my head or a knife to my throat. Why I went along with them as far as I did, I'll never know. Maybe it was the path of least resistance. I've never been a fan of resistant paths.

Kevin whispered, "Thank God I cleaned up this car. And got rid of that grass."

The deputy eased out of his cruiser and waddled up the shoulder of the road. He was a big, red-faced, pear-shaped looking fella, the kind of guy who couldn't run more than thirty feet before dropping dead. If it hadn't been for the uniform and the mirrored sunglasses and gun on his hip he would've looked about as menacing as a pussy cat. He rapped sharply on the driver's-side glass.

Kevin rolled down the window and smiled nervously. "Evening, officer," he said in a surprisingly calm, deep voice, but he wasn't fooling anybody. I could see our reflections in the sunglasses. We looked like four twitchy bunny rabbits.

He leaned an arm on the roof of the Jeep. "Where you boys off to in such a gol' dang hurry?"

"Just stopping for some gas."

"Filling station ain't goin' nowheres." He talked like he had a mouth full of mush along with a chaw of tobacco. "Clocked y'all doin' thirty-six in a thirty."

Kevin said, "Oh, so the speed limit was thirty?"

"Was and is." The deputy studied us one by one. He was really working his nose hard trying to detect the smell of liquor or marijuana. Dennis, of course, smelled like he'd been soaking in booze for two days.

"Let's see your license and registration."

There went my anal sphincter again. It sure was getting a workout.

"No problem," Kevin said. He slid out his wallet and handed the officer his brand-new learner's permit. My hand would have been shaking so bad the permit would have been flapping around like a frightened goose, but Kevin seemed calm, cool and collected.

"I don't know where the registration is," Kevin said. "We're just borrowing this car from a friend."

"Don't say." The deputy squinted at the learner's permit. "Kevin Przzz...zy...przzz..."

He gave up trying to pronounce the name.

"This here is a learner's permit," he said. He looked us over again. "Ya know you're required to have an adult in the *vee*hicle with you at all times?"

"We were just going to the gas station."

"You already said that."

The deputy looked over the top of his sunglasses and his face puckered to a scowl. I kept glancing at Dennis out of the corner of my eye praying he wouldn't do anything crazy. Thank God he hadn't been driving. Almost certainly he would have tried to outrun the deputy and we would have all ended up dead in a ditch somewhere down the road.

"Where y'all from?"

It was right there on the learner's permit—Kevin's address—but I suppose this was a test.

"St. Louis," Kevin said.

"Big city boys. What brings y'all down here?"

"We've been on a camping trip."

The deputy nodded. "On your own or you got some adults with ya?"

"We've got one adult with us."

The deputy bent down and gave the front and back seats a cursory examination. "Don't reckon I see him."

"He's back at the house."

"I see. And he let you drive this 'ere *vee*hicle even though you ain't got a license?"

Maybe for the first time in his life Kevin was at a loss for words.

But not Dennis. "He don't know we took the car."

I could taste the panic on the back of my throat. What the hell was he doing? Hadn't we warned him to keep his big yap shut?

"He don't?" the cop said. "Why's that?"

"He was asleep."

The deputy frowned heavily. "He sure goes to bed early. It ain't but six o'clock."

"He wasn't feeling too good," Dennis said.

The deputy pushed his sunglasses up his nose. "What seems to be ailing him?"

Dennis shrugged his shoulders. "Probably too much sun."

"I see. Fella wasn't feelin' good so ya took off in his Jeep and figured you'd fill up his gas tank for him."

Kevin was staring daggers at Dennis. Dennis slumped back in his seat and glanced out the window like he was suddenly bored with the whole boring conversation.

"He doesn't mind if we take the car, sir," Kevin said. "And we were gonna get something to eat too. We haven't eaten today and we were starved."

The deputy nodded and sniffed at the air inside the cab. "Smells like you've had quite a bit to drink though."

"No sir," Kevin said. "I haven't had nothing to drink, sir."

I thought Kevin was overdoing it with the "yes sir, no sir" stuff. It sounded phony as a hangman's laugh, but I guess it was better to suck up to a cop than to piss him off.

A noise crackled over the deputy's handheld radio. He took the radio from his belt and mumbled something mushy into it. The dispatcher mumbled something about a code 11-80 and a horse trailer. I think. It was hard to follow. The dispatcher had a mouthful of mush too. The deputy said something back at her and put away his radio. He peered at us for a moment and snapped his fingers in Kevin's face. "Let's have them keys."

"Umm."

"Keys!"

Kevin drew the keys from the ignition and handed them to the deputy. He dropped them in his shirt pocket. "Tell whatever adult is in charge of you he can pick these up at the sheriff's office later tonight."

"But..." Dennis said. "What about our car?"

"I ain't got time to mess with ya right now so this here *vee*hicle is officially impounded by the Iron County Sheriff's Department." He nodded down the road in the direction of town. "There's a telephone at the filling station you was headed to."

"But there's no phone at our campsite," I said.

"Not my problem." The deputy breathed in heavily through his nose. "And don't lemme catch ya behind the wheel of this or any other *vee*hicle...not 'til ya get your Missourah state driver's license."

The deputy turned on his heels and tramped back down the shoulder. He eased into his cruiser and a moment later he pulled a one-eighty and the cruiser shot off down the road like a police rocket, siren wailing.

We sat in silence for a moment; all four of us struck speechless.

At length Kevin slammed the steering wheel with his fist. "Fuck!" he cried.

"This ain't good," I said.

"We were *so* close to getting away with it," James said.

"Will you quit your fucking crying?" Kevin said.

"Fuck you, asshole!"

"He knows," Dennis said.

Kevin turned and gave Dennis a look that was equal parts angry, annoyed, weary and exasperated. "What?" he cried.

"He knows what we did."

"What do you mean *we*?" I said.

"If he knew he'd have locked us up," Kevin said.

"He's playing with us," Dennis said. "Like a cat plays with a mouse."

"Will you shut the hell up?" Kevin said. "God, I've about had it with you! All of you. Bunch of psychos and crybabies."

Right then a caravan of Harley riders rumbled past, guys in their thirties, Vietnam vet-looking, with long hair and hefty biker bitches clinging to their black leather jackets. They seemed to have come out of nowhere. Like ghost riders.

And just like ghosts, they vanished over a rise in the road.

Without keys and air conditioning, it felt like a sauna in the Jeep. I rolled down my window. James and Dennis did likewise.

After a long minute, Dennis said, "Anybody know how to hotwire a car?"

"If anyone did, it would be you," I said.

Dennis glared at me, his eyes hooded with contempt. "What's that supposed to mean?"

"Nothing," I said. I honestly don't know why I kept talking.

Dennis let it go. He must have been more interested in drinking than fighting. He reached under his seat and drew out the pint of Wild Turkey and took a good long swallow. He wiped his mouth with the back of his hand and stared out the window.

"Holy shit," he said, "look at that."

I looked. Across the way was a barbed wire fence with big wooden posts and hanging on the fence was a scarecrow fashioned out of twigs and sticks and some kind of purple overcoat with a big leathery face and black hollow eyes and a floppy gray hat. A scarecrow designed not so much to scare birds than to traumatize humans.

The seconds ticked by.

"Well, there's no point sitting here like a bunch of dopes," Kevin said. He eased out of the driver's side and slammed the door behind him and began tramping down the shoulder of the highway in the direction of town.

The rest of us got out and followed.

CHAPTER 10

ALREADY THE LIGHT WAS DYING. We tramped in silence, single file down the two-lane blacktop into town, keeping to the shoulder, except for Dennis who kept straying into the southbound lane. Secretly, I hoped he'd wander into the path of a logging truck and that would be the end of it. Maybe then Kevin and James would come to their senses and we would go to the police or call Kevin's dad. But there's never a logging truck around when you need one. Dennis would take a swallow of Wild Turkey every few of minutes and pass the bottle down the line to the next person. At this point we were all feeling so rotten and hopeless that we no longer had qualms about drinking.

Up ahead a rusted water tower loomed over the town like an alien spacecraft from *The War of the Worlds*. Beyond the tower rose Iron Mountain, the highest point in the state. Mountain is an exaggeration. It's really a long green ridge amid some other long green ridges. Still, it's a sight to behold, unless you happen to be stranded on a highway in the middle of nowhere with a priest-killer and his accomplices.

We walked past the gas station and kept going until we reached the center of town, a little business district where most of the shops were closed for the night. We passed a grade school and a dime store and a couple of nondescript Protestant churches. We followed a sign to a bronze statue of a young Ulysses S. Grant flanked by a Catholic church and a duck pond, and we paused to read the plaque. A future war hero and U.S. president seemed out of place in Iron Mountain, Missouri, but Grant had been here all right. In 1861, guarding the vitally important iron ore shipments from the area mines. Evidently, Grant thought Iron Mountain a "most delightful place." I would have given it two and a half stars, tops. We left Old Sam there gazing stoically out over the duck pond and made our way down Main Street. We passed a Victorian funeral parlor and a honky-tonk called The Mule Lip and the True Value hardware where we'd bought the shovels and The Iron Skillet where we'd had lunch the day before, only now it seemed more like a month ago. The sheriff's office and the county lockup stood on Russell Street next to the courthouse, and we huddled on the sidewalk across the street trying not to look suspicious while we worked out our next move. We needed an adult to get the keys, preferably one who wasn't wanted by the cops, but there didn't seem to be any around. There wasn't anyone around but us.

Dennis plopped down on a wooden bench in front of a shuttered barber shop and drew the pint of whiskey to his lips. It was *The Andy Griffith Show* all over again, and Dennis was playing Otis Campbell, the town drunk, passed out in front of Floyd's Barber Shop. Right after Otis stabbed a preacher to death.

"Put that shit away," Kevin snapped at Dennis. "We're in enough trouble already."

Dennis took a final swallow and slipped the bottle into his back pocket. Then he stretched out and placed the Panama hat over his face like a bum taking a nap on a park bench.

"You're about as useful as tits on a nun," Kevin said.

Dennis let out a loud fart.

I shuffled a short distance down the street and sat down on the curb. James soon joined me and he spent the next five minutes wiping the lenses of his glasses with his dirty polo shirt, but that only made them dirtier. Kevin wandered over and sat down beside us, wearily rubbing his face with his hands. "Well, I'm open to suggestions," he said.

We studied the gutter silently.

"I'm fresh out of ideas," James said.

"I could call my brother," I said. "If he's home and he left right now he could be here in two or three hours."

"And then what?" Kevin said.

"Then he'll drive us home."

"And we just leave the Jeep here?" Kevin said. "That wasn't the plan."

"Yeah, well, your plan went in the crapper when you got pulled over for speeding."

Kevin gave me a savage look, but he let it go.

As for Dennis, none of this seemed to have any impact on him. He just lazed on that barber shop bench as if this was all somebody else's problem.

"I think we need a new plan," James said.

"Like what?" Kevin said. "Let's hear it. What's your brilliant plan?"

James didn't respond.

"Well?"

"I'm just saying…"

Kevin breathed in steadily and looked around. "We're sticking to my plan."

"This is stupid," I said. "There's no way we're gonna get those keys. What're we gonna to do, walk up to some random stranger and say, 'Could you go over to the sheriff's office and pretend you're a priest and get our keys for us?'"

"Why not?" Kevin said. "We got about seventy bucks left. We offer him half of that."

"Who's gonna do that for thirty-five bucks?"

"A poor, drunk hillbilly might," Kevin said.

"A poor, drunk hillbilly?" I said incredulously. "Your brilliant plan depends on the cooperation of a poor, drunk hillbilly?"

"You got a better idea?"

"*Anything* is a better idea!" I looked to see if Dennis was listening (he didn't appear to be) then I lowered my voice to a whisper. I tried to make my tone as sympathetic and reasonable as possible—like that would do any good. "Guys, look," I said. "We tried. We covered for him. We probably did more than anyone else would have done...and look where we are." I looked Kevin in the eye. "We knew this was never gonna work. The whole thing was crazy from the start. Now we need to call your dad."

Kevin's eyes narrowed on me like blades. "We've been over this, Doofus," he said. "It's too late anyway. He's already six feet under. What are we gonna do, go out there and dig him up? Take him to a carwash and hose him off?"

I swear the only reason he wouldn't listen to me was he didn't want to admit that I was right all along, and he was wrong.

Kevin got to his feet. "Do you know what's gonna happen when they find out you helped bury the body of a dead priest?"

I felt my chest begin to tighten in anger.

"If you're lucky they'll lock you up in juvie hall until you're eighteen. That's if you're lucky...Is that what you want? Spending your high school years locked up with a bunch of degenerates? Oh, and you can kiss college goodbye."

I was surprised Kevin thought I was smart enough to go to college. In any case that was not what I wanted. Not that I believed any of that would happen. I honestly didn't know what might happen. But I sure wasn't taking Kevin's word for it.

"Um, guys," James said.

"What?" Kevin snapped.

James nodded down the street at a blue Dodge pickup pulling up in front of The Mule Lip. A medley of Lynyrd Skynyrd's greatest hits seeped from the truck's open windows. Presently, a long and lanky dude eased out of the truck, glanced at us briefly, and strode into the bar.

"Our prayers have been answered," Kevin said. "A drunk hillbilly."

"How do you know he's drunk?" I said.

"If he ain't, he will be soon enough." Kevin rubbed his hands together and looked at me and James excitedly. "Who's going?"

"It's your brilliant idea," I said.

"Exactly. I come up with the brilliant ideas and you guys implement them."

I said, "That's not how it works."

Kevin shrugged his shoulders. "Okay, you come up with a brilliant idea and I'll make it happen. But the clock's ticking."

My lip curled. "How come you always get to make the rules?"

"Times up," Kevin said. "We go with my plan."

James turned to look at me. "Rock, paper, scissors?"

I drew a breath and let it out slowly. Then I headed for the tavern.

CHAPTER 11

A COUPLE OF good old boys were slamming beers around a vintage pool table. One put in a dip of Copenhagen and racked the balls while the other leaned on a stick, sucking on a Budweiser longneck. They were the only ones in the tavern save a short, shapeless gal in her thirties perched on a stool behind the bar sink, flipping idly through a women's magazine. The juke was silent; the only sounds in the place were the click of pool balls and the hum of coolers. There was no TV set over the bar. Probably hard to get stations way the hell out there. The closest station would have been in Cape Girardeau, a good seventy miles as the crow flies.

The two men shooting pool looked to be in their midtwenties, gaunt with long greasy hair and sideburns, both of them. One tall, one about a foot shorter. They gave me a cursory glance as I walked in. Not hostile, but not friendly either. It took all my willpower not to turn around and walk back out.

The bartender glanced up from her magazine and studied me briefly. My eyes were still growing accustomed to the darkness when she said, "Can I help you?"

I froze. "I, uh…"

The bartender stared at me, unblinking. "Looking for somebody?"

"No…I mean, not really."

"You gotta be twenty-one to be in here."

I nodded. Christ, I hadn't expected the dive would have a bouncer.

"He looks twenty-one to me," said one of the pool players. It wasn't the guy with the pickup, but the other one. He had on a black Pink Floyd T-shirt. *Dark Side of the Moon.* Like every teenage boy in the Seventies, I would have known that album cover anywhere.

His buddy said, "Shit, he's gotta be at least twenty-five."

"Dwayne, you're so full of shit your teeth are brown," the bartender said.

The guy in the Pink Floyd T-shirt laughed. "Naw, they're more greenish-yellow."

They were definitely hillbillies, though I couldn't tell if they were drunk yet. Drunk enough to do something stupid and illegal. I leaned in confidentially to the bartender and said, "I just need to ask those fellas something, if that's all right."

The bartender frowned and turned back to her sex quiz or whatever it was she was doing. I went over to the pool table and drew up a stool. I was feeling nervous and self conscious and I hadn't a clue what I was going to say.

The one called Dwayne worked the tip of a stick with a blue cube of chalk and took a long pull from his beer. He fixed his eyes on me and said in a long, lazy drawl, "What d'you want to ask us?"

There was no time to rehearse my spiel or screw up my courage. I lowered my voice so the bartender couldn't hear me, then I commenced rambling. "Well, um, me and my buddies, you see…they're outside, across the street…well, uh, the thing is this police officer, I mean deputy, took away our car keys and…"

Dwayne grinned. He had a big dip of tobacco packed behind his bottom lip. I'd never seen anyone dip tobacco before. You probably had to get a good hour and half outside of the city before you found tobacco chewers. He said, "A big fat fuck with orange hair?"

I nodded.

"Douglas," his buddy said.

"What'd he take your keys for?" Dwayne said. "You boys weren't drinking and driving?"

He slammed the green six-ball into a corner pocket. A real nice shot. He probably got a lot of practice in a boring small town like this.

"Nothing like that," I said. "We were just wondering if one of you wouldn't mind going over to the police station and getting our keys."

Dwayne circled the table studying his next shot. "Now that's a strange request. Don't you think that's a strange request, Glenn?"

"Highly strange."

"We'd pay you."

"How much?" Glenn said.

Dwayne said, "You still ain't told us why Douglas took your keys."

"Well, we were sorta driving on a learner's permit."

"That ain't a crime."

"Without an adult."

They both laughed at that. "Where you boys from?" Dwayne said.

I said I was from south St. Louis and there were three more of us across the street.

"That's an awful long joyride," he said.

I didn't know what to say to that. I didn't want to get into the whole thing about our adult chaperone and how one of us had stabbed him forty times. So I took what Dwayne had said about a joy ride and made up a quick, simple story on the spot. I said my folks were out of town and the four of us got a wild hair and drove my dad's old Jeep down here to go canoeing. I thought the story sounded halfway believable. I just had to remember to clue in the others so we'd have our stories straight.

Dwayne spit into a paper cup and laughed and shook his head. "Sounds like some of the dumb shit I woulda done when I was your age."

"Or last week," Glenn said.

Dwayne grinned and took careful aim at the five-ball. "One question. Why would the cops give me the keys? I ain't exactly a stranger 'round the jailhouse. They know that ain't my *vee*hicle."

"Or mine," Glenn said.

"The deputy just said we needed an adult to get the keys back. He didn't say which adult."

"He probably meant one of y'all's parents."

I rubbed the back of my neck. "It's worth a try. What d'you got to lose?"

Dwayne took another drink of his beer. "I don't guess there's anything illegal about it. All they can say is no."

He looked at Glenn and Glenn shrugged. "Don't ask me."

Dwayne straightened and studied the lay of the table. He still seemed hesitant. "I don't know. I'm kinda busy kicking this hillbilly's ass right now."

I got up from the stool. "We can pay you."

"Yeah, you said that," Dwayne said. "How much are we talking?"

I figured he wouldn't accept the first figure I threw out, so I low-balled him. "Twenty-five bucks."

"Shiiiiiit," Dwayne said. "I wouldn't cross the street for twenty-five bucks."

I wasn't in the mood to dicker. "Fifty then?"

"I ain't getting within a hundred feet of the sheriff's office," Glenn said.

Dwayne winked at me. "Ol' Glenn just got out of the pokey last week. Sheriff promised he'd keep his dinner warm for him."

Glenn scowled. "That ain't nobody's business."

Dwayne blew his next shot, the two-ball in the side pocket. He scrubbed his hand over his face and said, "Let's see the fifty."

"I don't have it on me. But I can get it."

"Uh-huh." Dwayne spat into his paper cup. "It's fifty bucks whether they give me the keys or not."

"Oh," I said. I wasn't sure Dennis and Kevin would go for that. If not, I guess they could find their own "drunk hillbilly."

I turned and hurried outside.

The street was empty. It was the emptiest street I had ever seen. Where the hell had they gone off to? I glanced up and down the empty storefronts. Nothing. Not a peep. I fought a rising panic and set off down the sidewalk toward the cafe. They couldn't possibly have run off and left me behind, could they? Caught a ride with someone headed to St. Louis?

No, they were dead-set on getting the Jeep back.

Maybe they'd been arrested. Maybe the sheriff saw them loitering out front of the police station and figured they'd come to turn themselves in so he went out and rounded them up. You tend to have all kinds of ridiculous thoughts when you are panicking. At least I do.

Then I turned a corner and saw the three of them standing bunched in the middle of the street. I heaved a sigh of relief. "I think I found somebody!"

It was like they didn't hear me. It turned out the three of them were huddled around a dead opossum. The opossum looked like it had been run over by a steamroller two or three times. In death, it wore a creepy possumy grin on its face. Dennis had a hickory twig and he was poking the opossum in the ass with it.

"What're you doing?" I said.

"Told you he ain't dead," Dennis said.

"Did you hear what I said? I found somebody to get the keys."

"He's playing possum," Dennis said.

"You're crazy," Kevin said. "He's flat as a pancake. He's got flies and shit all over him."

"So do you," Dennis said. He poked the opossum in the eye with the twig. The opossum didn't twitch.

"Told you," Kevin said.

Dennis jammed his hands deep into his pockets. "I bet the minute we leave he's gonna get up and start laughing at us."

"Ten bucks says he don't," Kevin said.

I threw up my hands exasperatedly. "He wants fifty bucks!"

Kevin stared at me. "Who?"

"The fella in the bar."

"What fella in what bar?" Dennis said, and turned his attention back to the roadkill.

"He said he'll get the keys, but he wants fifty bucks."

"Screw that," Dennis said. He sniffed the pokey end of the twig and made a disgusted face.

"You got a better idea?"

James said, "Let's just give him the money and get it over with."

"Easy for you to say. It ain't your money," Dennis said.

"It ain't yours either!" I said.

Dennis turned on me and brandished the stick like a fencer wielding a foil. "Possession is nine-tenths of the law, motherfucker," he said. He poked me a few times with the twig. Not hard, but it was gross. It had been in a dead opossum's ass. Then he flung the twig as far as he could down the street.

"Let's go see this hillbilly," Kevin said.

Our leader had spoken. We turned and headed back to the tavern.

The town of Iron Mountain had already rolled up its sidewalks. Everything on Main and Russell streets except The Mule Lip and the sheriff's office had gone dark. Dennis picked up a stone and chucked it down the street. It skipped a few times and ricocheted loudly off the door of the blue pickup. "Man, I'm glad I don't live in this shit town," Dennis said. "Probably nothing to do here but bang your sister. Or your goat if you ain't got a sister."

"I'd bang a goat before I'd touch *your* sister," Kevin said.

"Lucky for me I ain't got a sister or a goat," Dennis said.

"Real intellectually stimulating conversation," I said.

"Listen to Doofus," Dennis laughed. "We might have to start calling him Poindexter."

We walked past the café and the hardware store.

"I say we go back and hotwire the Jeep," Dennis said.

"You already said that," Kevin said. "And you still don't know how to do it."

"I could figure it out. I saw it done once. All you gotta do is connect the thingamajig—"

"You mean the whatchamacallit?" Kevin said disgustedly.

"Starter wires…in the steering column."

"Which ones are those?" I said.

"The red ones. No, wait, the green ones."

"I'm pretty sure there's more to it than that," Kevin said.

"No shit," Dennis said. "You gotta connect the power wires, too." He thought about that. "Maybe those are the red ones."

I wasn't surprised that Dennis knew just enough about hotwiring a car to fry the battery. I cleared my throat loudly. "So, are we gonna give this guy fifty bucks, or are we gonna stand around here with our dicks in our hands?"

"Tell him he can have twenty," Dennis said.

"He won't do it for twenty! He already turned down twenty-five!"

James studied Dennis for a moment. "How much do we got left? There was like a hundred bucks in there."

"It wasn't that much," Dennis said. "And the shovels and cleaning supplies cost about twenty and we need something for gas and food."

"We can eat when we get home," I snapped. "And gas ain't gonna be more than ten bucks."

We passed a State Farm Insurance office with a yellow-and-black GO TIGERS! sign in the window. Dennis told us to wait a minute then he turned and ran back the way we'd come.

"For chrissake, now where's he going?" I said.

"Possum check," Kevin said.

"You've gotta be shitting me."

Dennis stopped at the corner. His shoulders slumped and he jammed his hands in his pockets and turned and shuffled back, kicking at stones.

"Ha! You owe me ten bucks," Kevin cried. "And not Father Ted's money."

"I coulda swore he was playing possum," Dennis said.

Nobody seemed in a hurry to do anything except chuck stones and poke dead opossums in the ass. Worst of all, I resented having to be the voice of reason, especially when I was completely opposed to what we were doing.

"If we don't give him the money now he's gonna change his mind or leave or ask for another twenty," I said. "Then what're we gonna do?"

Dennis took off the Panama hat and fanned himself with it. "Offer him twenty-five."

"You ain't listening!" I said. "He already said no to twenty-five. He wants fifty."

"Thirty then," Dennis said.

I threw up my hands. "You're welcome to tell him whatever." I nodded toward the front doors of The Mule Lip. "He's in there, shooting pool. The tall one in the Queen shirt."

"Fine," Dennis said. He drew the wallet from his back pocket and peeled off fifty bucks. Then he rolled up the money and held it out to me. I reached for it, but of course at the last moment he yanked it away. "Make sure he ain't taking us for a ride."

I didn't tell them he was going to keep the money even if he didn't get the keys. With any luck it wouldn't come up.

Dennis said, "Tell him you'll give him half now and half when we get the keys." He hesitated. "Or better yet, tell him he's got to hand over *his* car keys. When he gets our keys we trade—keys for keys."

"He's not gonna agree to that."

"If he wants the fifty bucks he will."

"Just give me the cash."

Dennis handed me the bills and I pocketed the fifty and headed back to the bar.

DWAYNE AND GLENN were milling around the jukebox, squabbling over which songs to punch in. I cleared my throat loudly a few times until I got their attention. Glenn turned and gave me a look.

"Well, look who it is."

"Didn't think you were coming back," Dwayne said. He dropped a handful of dimes into the coin slot.

"I got it," I said. "The whole fifty." I drew out the roll of bills and held it out to him. I wasn't about to give him half of the fifty or ask for his keys. That would've been a waste of time and it might have squelched the whole deal.

The bartender looked up from her magazine. "What's that for?"

"It ain't got nothing to do with you, Doreen," Dwayne said.

Doreen frowned and set down the magazine and got to her feet. "You know how I feel about illegal activities in my bar."

"Then maybe you oughta quit stealing from the till and watering down the booze," Glenn said.

"That ain't funny, Glenn Marquardt. Your dumbass jokes is how rumors get started."

"Weren't no joke."

Dwayne crammed the roll of bills into his jeans pocket and showed me a pair of raised eyebrows, as if to say, *Women, can't live with 'em...*

Then he turned back to the barmaid. "If you don't trust me, come over to the window and watch. I'm going over to the sheriff's office. Now how likely is it I'm doing something illegal over there?"

"I wouldn't put nothing past you, Dwayne Lee Akers."

Dwayne laughed and winked at me. "See what happens when you grow up in a small town? Folks know you too well." He strode over to the bar and set his longneck on the counter. "Put this on ice, will you, hon?" he said. "I'll be back in five minutes."

"Hell no, I ain't putting that in my clean ice."

"Clean ice! My asshole's cleaner than that ice."

Glenn punched in some more numbers on the juke. "Don't be calling over here asking me to bail your ass out," he said.

Some loud rock tune I didn't recognize came on. Sounded like Southern rock. Molly Hatchet, maybe. Or Blackfoot. It was hard to keep them straight.

"Godammit, I'm gonna miss my song," Dwayne said. He turned and gave me a distracted look. "Come on, city boy, let's get this over with."

We left the bar and were met on the sidewalk by Dennis, Kevin and James. Dwayne took a moment to look over the four of us. He seemed unimpressed by what he saw.

He said, "So where's this alleged *vee*hicle these keys go to?"

I said, "It's just off Highway 72, on the road into town, not far from the Shell station."

Dennis came up behind me and hissed in my ear: "Did you get his keys like I told you?"

Dwayne looked at me a moment as if to say, *What the hell's he talking about?* Then he let it drop. "So whose *vee*hicle is it again?"

My stomach knotted. He was testing us and I hadn't had a chance to tell the others my story—the one about it being my dad's car.

"What's it matter?" Dennis said.

"It matters 'cause I want to know what I'm getting myself into. And if I think you're lying to me I will walk away *and* keep the fifty bucks, so you punks better not be lying to me."

"I told you to get his keys!" Dennis cried.

Dwayne stopped, his eyes narrowing as he studied me. "What the hell's his problem?"

"Never mind him," I said.

Kevin spoke then. "It's my dad's car."

Dwayne grinned and nodded at me. "Yeah? Well, this one here said it's *his* dad's car. One of y'all's feeding me a bowl of bullshit."

"We're brothers," I blurted out. I wasn't sure where that had come from. Only after I had said it did I think about whether it made any sense.

It didn't really.

"Twins?" Dwayne said. "You two? You don't look anything like—"

"Stepbrothers," Kevin said.

Wow. Fast thinking on Kevin's part. Maybe he wasn't as dumb as I thought he was.

Dwayne smiled condescendingly. "You're shitty liars," he said. After a moment, he shook his head. "Well, let's get them keys before my beer gets warm."

CHAPTER 12

YOU BOYS WAIT HERE," Dwayne said. "If I ain't out in ten minutes, I'd beat it if I was you."

The four of us shared a look of panic. "We'd rather go with you," Kevin said.

"People in hell want a glass of ice water," Dwayne said. "No sir, it's my way or the highway."

Kevin grumbled, but he backed down.

Dwayne crossed the street and climbed the steps to the sheriff's office. He glanced over his shoulder and gave us a look, but I couldn't tell what the look meant. I hoped it didn't mean, *Suckers!*

Along Main Street the streetlamps were blinking on. There was probably less than fifteen minutes of daylight remaining. Dennis drew out the pint of Wild Turkey and we passed it around. I was getting used to the taste; it didn't burn as bad as it had the first couple of times. And I liked the feeling it was giving me. Like there was no point in worrying. Like who the hell cares what happens anyway?

We sat on the barber shop bench and passed the bottle back and forth like winos-in-training and kept our eyes on the doors to the sheriff's office. Several long minutes passed and nothing happened.

"We should've gone with him," James said. "What if he

ducks out the back way and steals the Jeep?"

"Then we steal his pickup," Dennis said.

I glanced down the street toward the bar. The Dodge was still parked out front.

"How're we gonna do that without keys?" James said.

"We hotwire it," Dennis said.

"Grand theft auto," I said. "About the only crime we haven't committed yet."

We sat in silence for a while longer, listening to the crickets and the muffled rock music from the tavern.

"Five churches," James said.

"What?" Kevin said.

"I count five houses of worship on this street. Five churches and one bar."

"What better way to spend a summer night," Kevin said. "Counting country churches."

At that moment the door to the sheriff's office banged opened and Dwayne strode out dangling the keys in front of his face and grinning like the village idiot.

My heart did a little backflip. I don't think any of us really believed we'd get away with it.

Dwayne said, "Easiest fifty bucks I ever made."

"Did they give you any trouble?" Kevin said.

"Nah. The only one on duty was Sylvia Denton and I just buttered her up, asked her if she'd gotten her hair done, asked after her family. Now if it had been Pee Wee Nichols on duty we'd have been up shits creek. That fucker hates my guts ever since I gave his little sister the clap. Hell, that's ancient history." Dwanye's gaze shifted to me. "I guess you get these." He tossed me the keys. "Oh, and word to the wise. When y'all resume your little joyride, remember the pigs like to hide behind the Pentecostal church out by the highway."

"We know," I said.

"That's right." He laughed shortly. "Welp, been nice doing business with you." Then he turned and hurried down the street toward The Mule Lip.

"Hang on!" Kevin said.

Dwayne stopped and looked hesitantly over his shoulder. "Sorry boys, our business is completed."

"For fifty bucks you could at least give us a ride to our car."

Dwayne shook his head. "No dice," he said. "That weren't part of the deal. Next time read the fine print."

"Come on, man. We've had a shitty day and it's like a five-mile hike to the Jeep."

"It ain't that far and besides it ain't my fucking problem." He moved off toward the bar.

"How about for a pint of vodka?"

"No way," Dennis cried. "That shit's mine!"

Dwayne stopped. He turned and gave us a curious stare. "I knew I smelled booze," he said. "Where'd you punks get a bottle of vodka?"

"A pint for a ride to our car," Kevin said. "Deal?"

"What kind of vodka?"

"The best."

"Smirnoff," James said.

Dwayne made a face. "I don't know. I usually stick to Tennessee whiskey."

"Well, we only got vodka," Kevin said.

Dwayne considered the offer for some little time. "Let's see it."

"It's in the Jeep," Kevin said.

"Ha! Nice try. You must think I'm one of them dumbass hillbillies."

"We're serious," Kevin said. "It's in the Jeep. Dennis's got a pint of Wild Turkey, but there ain't much left. But you're welcome to that, too."

"No he ain't!" Dennis cried.

"Wild Turkey, eh?" Dwayne felt with his hand along the line of his jaw. "Where'd you get all that booze anyway?"

"Same place we got the car," Kevin said.

Dwayne smiled at that. "Borrowed it from your stepdad, huh?"

Kevin nodded.

Dwayne looked thoughtful for a moment, then his eyes focused back on Kevin. "I guess I could keep the vodka for emergencies," he said. "All right, but give me back the keys. If you're lying to me I'm keeping them."

I dug the keys out of my pocket and tossed them to Dwayne.

"That's my blue truck in front of the tavern. Some of you'll have to ride in the back. And don't touch nothing in my toolbox."

We made our way to the pickup. Dennis and Kevin got into the front seat and James and I climbed into the bed. We headed out of town, rolling west toward Highway 72.

CHAPTER 13

THE PICKUP SLOWED as we neared the highway. We pulled over at the spot where the deputy had stopped us. I could see the Shell sign rising over the hill. But there was no sign of the Jeep.

In vain, we drove up and down the same forlorn stretch of highway. The Jeep was gone.

Dwayne pulled over to the shoulder and James and I climbed out of the bed and went to see what was going on. Walking up, I heard Dwayne say, "Weeeeeell shit. So much for my vodka." Then, "Y'all sure are some unlucky sonsabitches. I hope that bad luck don't rub off on me."

"What's going on?" James said. "Where's the Jeep?"

"Sheriff's office probably had it towed," Dwayne said. "They got a nice little business towing out-of-town *vee*hicles. It's how the bastards get most of their revenue. That and speed traps. It's one hell of a racket." He reached for a tin of Copenhagen on the dashboard. He put a dip behind his lower lip and leaned out the window and spit onto the gravel shoulder. "Welp, this is where we say goodbye."

"Towed where?" Kevin said.

"Hmm?"

"Where'd they tow it to?"

"They got a fenced-in lot behind the sheriff's office for impounded *vee*hicles. Looks like a goddamn used car lot. Hope you boys got more cash than you're letting on."

"Why?" I said.

"You're gonna have to pay tow charges. Probably some other charges, too."

Kevin said, "How much will that be?"

Dwayne shrugged. "Cost this one ol' boy I know twenty-five bucks. His truck died on the way into work and a deputy had it towed—and he was a local." He chuckled at the thought. "He went to the sheriff's office and totally lost his shit. Started throwing chairs against the protective glass. Glass didn't break but the chairs did. They ended up locking his ass up for a month for property damage and assaulting a police officer, even though the cops were all in the next room. Lost his job and his apartment and then his girlfriend left him." He gave me a look. "That little fella, Glenn. You met him back at the bar."

He spat on the ground and peered at the four of us for a moment. Then he sadly shook his head. "Ah hell, get in," he said. "We'll swing by the lot and see if your Jeep's there. It's on the way. But that's it. No more free rides."

It was full-on dusk when we got back to town. Dwayne drove around to the back of the sheriff's office. There was a gravel lot back there, fenced in with old chain link and razor wire and illuminated by the sick yellow glow of a vapor light. I saw a red Trans Am with two flat tires and a cracked windshield, and a couple of pickups and a few other vehicles, but the Franklin's Jeep wasn't among them. Dwayne put the truck in park and left it idling. James and I hopped out of the bed and went around to the driver's door.

"So where is it?" Kevin said. "What happened to it?"

"Looks to me like somebody beat the cops to it."

"What do you mean somebody else?" Kevin said. "Who?"

Dwayne reached across Kevin and Dennis and opened the passenger door for them. "If I was you boys I'd go in there and talk to the sheriff. 'Course there's a excellent chance he's in on it, too." He straightened behind the wheel. "Now out you go."

Kevin scootched out of the cab. Dennis followed hesitantly.

"In on what?" Kevin said.

Dwayne spat out the window. "Well now, that's hard to say. But if that Jeep's where I think it is, you may as well forget about it."

James said, "Where do you think it is?"

"Gone. Cut up in a thousand pieces."

We all looked at each other for a second. *What the hell was that supposed to mean?*

"Boys, it's been real, and it's been fun, but it hasn't been *real* fun. Now I got a warm beer waiting for me back at The Mule Lip. Good luck whatever you decide."

Dwayne's arm rested on the windowsill and I latched on to it. "You can't just leave us here!"

Dwayne looked at my hand on his arm. It wasn't a friendly look. "Excuse me?"

"Can't you at least drop us at our campsite?"

"You fellas got me confused with a taxi driver. This here's where we part ways."

He shook my hand off, then he went into his pocket and tossed me the keys to the Jeep. "Yours, I believe."

I stood there looking blankly at the set of keys. Kevin snatched them out of my hands and pushed me out of the way. "Come on, man," he said. "You ain't gonna make us walk all that way in the dark. We don't even know where our campsite is. We'll be wandering up and down the highway 'til morning."

"God, you're a bunch of whiny-ass bitches," Dwayne said. "How many times do I gotta tell you this ain't my problem."

"Just to the campsite," I pleaded.

"Not happenin'."

"Come on, man!"

Dwayne shook his head.

It got real quiet for a moment. He put the truck into gear, but he didn't drive off. Instead he slowly lowered his head until his forehead thumped against the steering wheel. "Awww hell, I must've gone soft in the head. But *goddamn* it, this is it. I mean it this time."

"Cool!" I said.

Before he could change his mind, James and I climbed into the bed of the pickup. Kevin and Dennis slipped back into the cab.

We drove for some fifteen or twenty minutes on dark, winding backroads. White-tailed deer by the dozens lined the highway and studied us as we passed. Over an Allman Brothers eight-track tape, I could hear Dennis and Kevin bickering about the right way to the ranch house, and Dwayne telling them to quit arguing, they were giving him a headache. I didn't recognize a single thing we passed, but then I didn't really expect to.

Another fifteen minutes came and went. By then I knew we'd never find the house. It was just one more letdown in a long line of disappointments. A few minutes later we pulled over by an unmarked dirt road. As far as I could tell, we were nowhere near the house. Or any other place, for that matter.

Dwayne turned down the Allman Brothers and switched off the headlights and we sat there idling in the dark. James and I climbed wearily out of the bed and went around to the front.

"Don't tell me we're lost," James said.

"I ain't lost," Dwayne said. "I know exactly where I am, and I don't like it one bit." He shot a stream of tobacco juice out the window and turned to Dennis and Kevin. "Remember what I said. When them Sikas start torturing your asses don't you fucking tell them I brung you out here."

Kevin widened his gaze to take in me and James. "He thinks the Jeep might be here."

I glanced up and down the county road. I didn't see anything but dark, endless highway and pine forest and a lonesome dirt road trailing off into the woods. Meanwhile the wind was picking up, riffling the shortleaf pines by the side of the road. The air had a wet smell to it like stale beet soup and I felt the first splash of rain on my face. The temperature was dropping too, like it does when a cold front blows in. It almost felt good after a hot, sunburnt afternoon.

"Where?" I said.

"He says there's a chop shop back in there." He turned to Dwayne. "How far is it?"

"Five hundred yards, give or take."

"Give or take what?"

"You want me to get out my tape measure?"

What the hell was a chop shop? It sounded like a place where you'd buy cuts of meat, or maybe Chinese food. And that seemed unlikely out here. Everything seemed unlikely out here, except maybe getting hit by a logging truck.

I drew Kevin aside. "What's he mean…about us being tortured?"

Dwayne leaned across Kevin and Dennis and pushed open the passenger side door. "Y'all can have this conversation after exiting my truck. I don't want to be sitting here when one of them Sikas drives up."

"Them the assholes that stole our Jeep?" Kevin said.

"You mean stole the Jeep you stole from your stepdad?" Dwayne said. "Very likely. They probably got it chopped up into a hundred pieces by now. Now out you go."

Kevin and Dennis eased out of the pickup. Kevin paused and leaned into the window. "What if we give you another twenty bucks and all the liquor we got left? Will you take us out there? That's seventy bucks total and enough booze to stay drunk for a week."

Dwayne barked out a laugh. "Twenty bucks to get my dick blown off? No thank you."

"You ain't scared, are you?" Kevin said.

"What I *am* is tired of foolin' with a bunch of ignorant city kids."

Kevin turned to me and James and said, "Check your pockets. See how much cash we can come up with."

"A waste of time," Dwayne snapped. "You're talking about a kamikaze mission."

I still had six bucks and some change. Kevin said he only had four, which was a goddamn lie. James had the most, fifteen dollars. Dennis said he didn't have anything but the twenty in Father Ted's wallet and we needed that for gas...assuming we got the Jeep back.

Kevin collected our money. "That's another twenty-five." He held the roll out to Dwayne. "That and all the liquor we got left. What d'ya say?"

More raindrops fell. Big ones falling steadily. Dwayne shook his head wearily. "Any minute it's gonna start raining like a tall horse pissing on a flat rock." He turned off the stereo and drummed his fingertips absently on the steering wheel. "Tell you what I'll do. I'll drive you back to wherever you're staying. No charge. Be worth it not to have your deaths on my conscience."

For a moment I almost got my hopes up; maybe this endless nightmare would soon be over.

I should have known better. Kevin and Dennis had no interest in going back to the campsite.

Dwayne shrugged and shook his head sadly. "Okay. Your funerals." He put the truck into drive, but kept his foot on the brake. "I'm gonna give you one more piece of advice, though I don't expect you'll take it. Stay downwind. Them fellas got some nasty-ass pit bulls that'll rip your ballsack off if they get half a chance." He shook his head again as if to say, *Poor dumb sumsabitches.* Then he stepped on the gas and the tires spun and threw up some dust and gravel and the truck sped away.

We watched until the pickup's taillights were swallowed up by the night. Thunder rolled over the valley.

James turned to Kevin and Dennis. "Somebody wanna tell me what's going on?"

"We're gonna get the Jeep back, what d'ya think?" Kevin said.

"How do we even know it's here?" I said.

Dennis drew the pint of Wild Turkey from his pocket and drained the last of it. "We don't," he said. He tossed the empty across the highway into a line of trees. "But there's only one way to find out."

CHAPTER 14

WE COULDN'T SEE for shit. The rain clouds and dense tree canopy blocked out all the moonlight and stars, but on the plus side, the leaves kept off most of the rain. We stumbled on ruts and slipped on stones and tripped over downed branches. If you've ever tried to follow a narrow dirt road through the woods at night without a light (we'd left James's flashlight in the Jeep) you know what it's like. The occasional whack in the face from a tree limb is the only way to know you've strayed from the path. Meanwhile the temperature was dropping fast like it does when it's cloudy and country dark. Dennis flicked on a cigarette lighter but it would have taken a thousand lighters to make a dent in that darkness. After a few minutes of bumping into trees and getting whacked in the face by twigs, a dull yellowish light appeared in the distance. The chop shop. It had to be. At that same moment a rumble rose up behind us and the woods lit up like high noon on a cloudless day. The four of us started and whirled around. A huge truck—almost like the ones with the gargantuan wheels you'd see in those late-night ads on local TV crushing rows of junk cars (*"A Monster Motorsports Spectacular! Beeeee Theeere!"*)—came rumbling up the road, shaking the ground beneath our feet.

"Hit the dirt!" Kevin cried.

We dove for cover...only there wasn't any cover. No thick

trees or underbrush or large rocks. Nothing. We made do by dropping to the ground and lying motionless with our heads down in the wet leaves and the poison oak and poison sumac. The V-8 engine thundered like a freight train as the big truck rumbled by. The truck didn't slow or stop, so whoever it was must not have seen us.

I lay in those wet leaves a good, long time, long after the danger passed, wondering how the hell I'd ended up here, in a cold dark forest in the drizzling rain, trying to steal someone else's Jeep back from a gang of homicidal hillbillies?

How, Lord?

I found myself thinking about my mom and dad back in the comfort of our little craftsman bungalow in the city and how they had insisted I go on this trip. *"It'll be fun,"* they said. *"A nice adventure with your friends. It'll be good for you to get out of the city and spend some time in the great outdoors."* And I promised myself that if I somehow managed to survive this *nice outdoor adventure*, I would never again take my parents' advice. Never.

"Did you see the size of that thing?" Kevin said.

"Fucking monster truck," Dennis said.

"No it wasn't. It was just a lifted pickup with off-road tires." James said, "You'd need a ladder to get up in it."

On and on they went, arguing about what kind of truck it was.

I got to my feet and fell in behind them, feeling cold and angry and disgusted and on the verge of tears. We tramped on miserably in the drizzling rain. As the light grew brighter it was easier to keep to the road and before long we could make out the sound of barking dogs over the rumbling hum of diesel generators. Suddenly we came to a fork in the road. Ahead lay the entrance to the chop shop or whatever it was called, an iron gate with a heavy chain across it. That was a non-starter. Curving off the left was a faint footpath that led around the enclosure. We took the footpath, marching single-file like a band of sad, hopelessly lost Indians. My clothes felt like rags soaked in buckets of ice water and my teeth chattered like a pair of those wind-up dentures you buy at the novelty store.

As we trudged on, we studied the walls of the enclosure. Eight-foot-high sections fashioned from rusted sheet metal and other bits of discarded junk. We clambered up a small incline to a rocky outcropping where we could see inside the chop shop. There were a couple of trailers, a flatbed loaded with axles, and four metal buildings that looked right at home in the forests of Iron County. On the far side of the lot sat a beat-to-hell 1940s school bus and a twelve-foot-high mound of used tires. Random auto parts lay scattered about. Everything was lit up by light towers connected to mobile diesel generators, the kind you see at night on highway construction sites—which is probably where they were stolen from. There were a lot of them and the din was low and constant. Everywhere there were vehicles in various stages of dismemberment. One of every make and model, it seemed, but a Jeep Wagoneer.

The monster truck stopped in front of one of the buildings and sat there idling noisily. I counted four vicious-looking pit bulls sniffing around the lot looking for something to rip to shreds. If some poor dumb auto parts thief was unlucky enough to get past the sheet-metal fence he'd be in for a nice surprise.

A lightning flash cut through the wooded darkness, and on its heels came a thunderclap so loud and strong it shook the rocks we stood on.

The thunder-echo faded slowly away.

"I don't see it," I said.

"Well shit," Kevin said.

I glanced at James. He looked like he'd kept it together for as long as he could. He choked back a sob and, at the risk of pissing off Kevin, said, "Now what do we do?"

Personally, I didn't mind the Jeep not being there. If it *had* been there Kevin would have wanted to do something crazy stupid to get it back and we would have been either torn to shreds by pit bulls or shot to pieces by car thieves.

Actually, getting shot sounded quicker and less painful.

We squatted on the wet, mossy outcropping and took stock. There was no Jeep and we were stranded in a forest somewhere in the Ozark foothills and the night was pitch-black and cold and rainy and we had no idea where we were or how to get back to our house, let alone how to get back to St. Louis.

And I almost forgot. The police were probably looking for us, too, regarding a recent homicide.

"Can we go now?" I said in my best non-whiny voice, which still sounded way-too whiny to my ears.

"Go where?" Kevin said. "Where are we gonna go?"

"Well there's no point staying here," James said. "We c-c-could get out of the rain at least."

"I could sure use a pint of Wild Turkey and a cigarette," Dennis said.

There was movement inside the walls. We went deathly quiet as a tall, wiry figure climbed out of the truck. He carried a couple of pizza-sized boxes and a twelve-pack of beer and went around the side of one of the metal buildings, the four yapping, nipping pitbulls at his heels.

"Why didn't you tell your friend to wait 'til we found out if the Jeep was here," Kevin asked me.

"Yeah, this is all my fault." I didn't bother pointing out that Dwayne wasn't my friend or that he would have laughed in my face if I'd asked him to wait. I wiped a strand of wet hair out of my eyes and turned to Dennis. "You think we're within walking distance of your uncle's place?"

Dennis shrugged. "I ain't got a dog-fucking clue where we are."

Somewhere above us an owl hooted. Mr. Owl sounded cold, wet and miserable too.

"We c-c-could hitchhike," James said, his teeth chattering like castanets. "Somebody'd pick us up eventually. Maybe they'd drop us off in town. We might be able to find our way back to the c-c-camp site from there."

"And then what?" I said. I was shivering like a chihuahua taking a shit in a blizzard.

"At least we c-c-could get out of these wet clothes and get some sleep," James said.

I didn't want to go back to that goddamn shack. I wanted to go home, or, at the very least, to the sheriff's office. "And then what?" I said.

"I don't know! But it beats standing in the rain, saying 'And then what' over and over like a doofus!"

That hurt. I was used to Kevin and Dennis snapping at me, calling me names, but not James. It was feeling more and more like three against one.

Who was I kidding? It was always three against one. The more I thought about it, the more I was convinced I'd be better off on my own. I couldn't do any worse. I might even do better. Anything was better than staying with those dipshits.

What'd I have to lose?

"Screw this," I muttered. And before I could have second thoughts I clambered down from the rocks and started down the path into the pitch-black night.

"Doofus, where do you think you're going?" Kevin hissed at me.

"Home," I said, and I kept on going. "I don't care if I have to walk all the way to St. Louis. I ain't waiting around here another minute."

I moved on down the muddy path. Slowly, cautiously, because I couldn't see more than a few steps ahead of me, even with the remnant glow of the light towers. All the while slipping on wet leaves and tripping on ruts and getting smacked in the face by sharp branches. I felt that burning sensation in the back of my throat you get when everything seems hopeless and your eyes are boiling with hot tears, but I kept going. I wondered if they'd come after me, try to stop me, threaten me if I didn't come back. Gang up on me. Maybe even kill me. I stumbled over something, a rock or log, and fell on my hands and knees in the mud. A twig or something slashed across my cheek, drawing blood. But the thought of them bastards coming after me made me hurry to my feet and move on.

A light stopped me. It bounced up and down the path and from side to side. It wasn't big and bright like the headlights of a truck, more like someone shining a flashlight, searching the woods for someone or something. One of the Sikas, no doubt. I couldn't see anything to duck behind, so I turned and quickly retraced my steps, trying to feel my way along the path back to the others. Luckily, I hadn't gotten very far.

They must have seen the light too, because Kevin hissed at me. "Get down, Doofus!"

I scrambled up the slope where the others were and I flattened myself against the cold sandstone. My foot connected with someone or something.

"Oww! You kicked me in the face!"

My old buddy James. "Sorry," I said.

"Shut the hell up, you two!" Kevin hissed.

I put my head up for a look. The yellow light bobbed closer in the gray, misty drizzle. It was just one guy with a flashlight. No dogs. That was a relief. If things got hairy it was four against one. And at least one of us was a cold-blooded killer.

When he got about even with us he stopped suddenly and ran the light along the sheet metal fence. Then he aimed the light up at the outcropping, like he was looking right at us.

"Hey, it's your buddy!" Kevin whispered to me. "The guy who got our keys!"

"No it isn't," James said.

"It *is* him!" Dennis said.

I wasn't convinced it was Dwayne, but it didn't matter because Kevin called out: "Hey! Up here!"

The flashlight flitted over us. "There you are," he said. "I just about gave up." He hesitated. "They shoot any of your dumb asses yet?"

It was Dwayne all right. We crawled down the muddy slope to the footpath. One by one, Dwayne shone the flashlight's beam in our faces. We were all shivering limbs and chattering teeth.

"Not yet," James said. "But it's still early."

Dwayne blinked into the darkness. "Wait...weren't there four of you?"

I cocked my thumb toward the big slabs of gray rock. "Up there."

Dwayne's flashlight scanned the rocks until it found Dennis balanced on the ledge of the outcropping. He seemed to be studying something with great interest...something on the other side of the wall.

"How d'you like that, not a scratch on you," Dwayne said. "I figured this here would be a recovery mission. Brought four body bags for nothing." Then he looked at me. "So...is your *vee*hicle here?"

I shook my head. "Not unless they chopped it up already."

"I doubt it. Them hillbillies prefer stealing and drinking to working."

There was an extended silence. Then a radio went on in one of the garages and we caught the trail end of a Bad Company song. Then a power tool whirred and a sledgehammer clanked. It sounded like someone was busy.

"Come on, I'll drive you back to your campsite," Dwayne said, "like I should've done in the first place. Before we get fucking pneumonia."

This time no one objected. It wasn't the outcome they'd hoped for, but it sure beat freezing to death in the cold, damp woods.

Kevin called up to Dennis. "Come on, man, we're leaving."

While we waited for Dennis, we asked Dwayne why he had come back.

"Been asking myself the same question," he said, "the whole drive out here. Dwayne, why the fuck are you doing this?

Dwayne, them kids ain't none of your business. Dwayne, you ought to have your head examined." He scratched the back of his neck. "Guess I felt responsible for bringing you out here only to get murdered by them white trash sonsabitches. Or wander off the side of a cliff. Or freeze to death." He shook his head. "Dammit, I must be getting soft."

A streak of lightning lit up the woods for a fleeting second.

"I see it!" Dennis shouted.

We glanced up the slope, surprised by the urgency in Dennis's voice. He was dancing around on the rock outcropping like his feet were on fire and waving Father Ted's hat and gesturing toward the compound.

The color drained from Dwayne's face. "Somebody tell that idiot to shut up before them dogs hear him!"

Kevin and James scrambled halfway up the slope so they wouldn't have to shout. "Keep your voice down!" Kevin hissed.

"What do you see?" James said.

"The Jeep! I saw it."

"What?" Kevin cried. "Where'd you see it?"

Dennis waved a hand toward the ragged sheet-metal fence. "In there. One of them hicks opened a garage door and there it was."

"You're sure?" Kevin said.

"I'm gonna lie about this?"

"Now just hold on there," Dwayne said uneasily. "I did not come back here to get my dick blown off. Now y'all want a ride back to your campsite or not?"

"I do," I said.

Kevin turned and gave me a dark look. "What the hell good is that? We'll just be stranded out there, no car, no phone. No way home."

"Someone will come check on us eventually."

"Yeah, and then what? What're we gonna say about…" Kevin caught himself and his voice trailed off.

The sudden silence seemed to rankle Dwayne and he grew

animated. "About what?" he said. He strode up to Kevin and poked him sharply in the chest. "I knew there was something you punks weren't telling me. What *are* you gonna say about *what*?"

Dwayne glanced back and forth between us, but no one said a word. I glanced sideways at James. After me, he was the one least on board with the whole idiotic scheme. But he just slid his arms around his shoulders and shivered and stared down at his muddy sneakers.

Thunder echoed through the hills. When it grew quiet again, Dwayne said, "Fine, don't tell me. I don't give a good goddamn anyway…I'm cold and wet and tired of messing with you." He gave us one last look and clicked on the flashlight and moved off a short distance down the path before he stopped and called back over his shoulder. "You coming or not?"

"You don't understand," Kevin said. "We gotta get that Jeep back." His tone had totally lost its edge. It was like a little boy's voice now—the sound of a scared little kid who had done something wrong. "We don't have a choice."

Dwayne stared hard at Kevin, his lips pressed tight in a rigid smile. "In that case, you'd better get the sheriff out here before they chop it up like sliced baloney. I'd say you got about three, four hours tops."

"We told you, we can't do that!" Kevin said.

Dwayne switched off the flashlight. "Why the hell not? And you better tell me quick because I'm outta here in about ten seconds—with or without you."

We fell into a gloomy silence as the three of us exchanged sheepish glances.

Dwayne ran his hand across the sharp stubble on his cheek and slowly shook his head. "You know what? I don't care. I don't give a shit what you punks did. I should never have gotten involved with you in the first place." He turned on the flashlight again. "See you in the obituary pages." Then he turned and moved off down the path.

"Wait!" James said.

"What are you doing?" Kevin said.

"We need his help!"

"The hell we do! We just gotta wait until they leave. Then we go over the walls."

James stared. "So those dogs can tear us to pieces?"

Dwayne stopped, then he turned and laughed bitterly. "Leave? They ain't leaving. Not until sun-up, anyway. Sikas are nocturnal, like wolves and coyotes. Only more vicious."

"Then we'll wait 'til morning," Kevin said.

Dwayne studied us a moment, then his voice took on a more somber note. "I ain't coming back. You stay out here in this cold wet valley, you'll all be dead of exposure by morning. That's if them peckerwoods don't get you first."

We stood looking at each other, hugging ourselves and shivering violently in the cold rain. Thunder drummed in the distance.

"Tell him." It was Dennis. Suddenly he was right beside us, his voice solemn and subdued. A moment passed. "Go on!" His voice rang out sharply, echoing among the trees until it faded into the din of the generators.

The rain dripped. My teeth chattered. The thought of hypothermia was starting to scare me more than the Sikas. (I remembered reading once in the *Farmer's Almanac* that more people died of hypothermia in the summer than in the winter.) But telling this stranger that we'd—that *Dennis* had killed someone—our adult guardian, that just seemed crazy. And reckless. And unnecessary.

So naturally that's what we did.

"We didn't come down here alone," James said. "There was someone with us."

"You don't say?" Dwayne said. He didn't sound too surprised.

"A priest."

Dwayne gave us a blank stare. "Wait, you came down here

with a priest? Why the hell didn't he get your keys?"

The rain dripped steadily.

After a moment, Dennis said, "Cause he's dead."

Dwayne continued to stare at us, like he was holding out for the punchline. "That's a good reason," he said. Then, "And how did he die?"

"I stabbed the fucker," Dennis said.

Dwayne studied Dennis closely, his mouth a crooked smile. Then he let out a short, clipped laugh. "Okay, you wanna tell me why you stabbed him? Were his sermons too long?"

"It's not funny," James said.

"If you say so."

Kevin drew himself up and cut his eyes toward Dennis. "The sick son of a bitch was...molesting him."

After that it got real quiet. If not for the generators grinding away you would have thought the whole forest was holding its breath. I couldn't bear to meet Dennis's gaze so I kept my eyes fixed on the ground at my feet.

It was Dwayne who finally broke the silence. The grin on his face had collapsed and his eyes had grown wide. "Wait...you're serious?"

Kevin swallowed twice and said nothing. Then he gave a little nod.

For a long moment Dwayne stood there, frozen to the spot. Suddenly his whole manner changed and his voice turned husky with rage. "So, you're telling me...you got me mixed up in a homicide?"

"It was self-defense!" Dennis cried.

"That's still a homicide!"

We were silent, wondering if that was indeed true.

Then Dwayne scrubbed his hand over his face. "I cannot fucking believe this."

"What are you worried about?" Dennis said. "You ain't done nothing wrong. Nothing...criminal."

Dwayne whirled on Dennis. His jaw tightened and his fists

clenched white at the knuckles. "Oh no. Just accessory to murder after the fact. That ought to buy me twenty years in Jeff City."

"It wasn't murder!" Dennis shouted. "Jesus! How many times do we gotta say it?"

Kevin said, "Besides, you didn't know, so how can you be an accessory?"

"Well, I do now. So I guess I better get my dumb ass to the sheriff's office." He rolled his eyes. "Like them fuckers are gonna believe anything *I* say."

The rain thudded against the leaves. Inside one of the garages, a circular saw whined and screeched. I wondered if that was the whine of our Jeep being hacked to pieces.

Dwyane said, "If it was self-defense why didn't you go to the police?"

Kevin spoke up. "We were gonna. I mean, we were gonna tell my dad."

"Your dad? What is he, a lawyer?"

"He's a cop."

I almost spoke up. I almost said *no we weren't. We weren't going to tell anyone!* But I kept my mouth shut.

Dennis said, "But then these assholes stole our Jeep."

Dwayne said, "So you could've reported the dead priest and the stolen Jeep at the same time!"

"And what if they didn't believe us…about it being self-defense?" Dennis said. "How many people kill priests in self-defense?"

Dwayne said, "I give up. How many?"

"None!"

Dwayne breathed in heavily through his nose. "So instead of going to the cops you figured you'd drag me into your…" He paused while searching for the right words. "Your murder cover-up."

"We needed someone to get our keys," Kevin said.

"And my dumb ass just happened to be there."

JACKS FORK

Over the radio a Bob Seger song came on. *Night Moves.* Someone cranked up the volume. For one weird moment we all seemed to listen appreciatively to the opening verse: *I was a little too tall could've used a few pounds. Tight pants, points, hardly renown.* And when that verse ended, Dwayne's entire manner seemed to change again.

"Well...I guess I can't blame you too much for not going to the sheriff. Sumbitch's got a bad reputation for beating false confessions out of people. And not just hippies and niggers. No telling what he'd do to your punk asses."

Kevin gave me a smug look as if to say, *See, Doofus, I told you.*

Dwayne stared at Dennis with a puzzled frown. After a few seconds he said, "So what happened with this preacher? Was the fucker trying to bugger you or what?"

Dennis gave him a look that said, *Can we not go there?*

Dwayne waited. A long moment passed.

Out past the cornfields where the woods got heavy...

"So you knifed him?" Dwayne said.

Dennis looked away and held silent.

"Where is he now? The preacher?"

Kevin said, "In the woods by a cornfield. Near some old falling-down bridge."

"You just left him out there?"

Nobody said anything. Especially nothing about how we'd buried the evidence.

A moment ticked by. Dwayne literally looked like his head was going to explode. He squeezed his eyes shut and rubbed the back of his neck. "I still don't understand why you need that Jeep. Why can't you just call someone to come get you?"

Kevin said, "'Cause that sheriff is gonna come looking for us and when he does we'd prefer to be over the county line."

Dwayne stood there thinking about that. "Yeah well, if them Sikas catch you inside their compound you're gonna *wish* the sheriff caught you." He turned and gave Dennis a look like something important had just occurred to him. "Lemme ask you something. This preacher...he ever try anything like this before?"

Dennis made no reply.

Kevin and James and I exchanged nervous glances. I guess somewhere in the back of our minds we'd been wondering the same thing.

"Is that a yes?"

Dennis looked away.

"I asked you—"

"Yes, goddammit!"

I felt myself burn all along my nerve endings, like a jolt of electricity was running laps in my nervous system. "What the fuck?" I cried.

Dwayne looked at Dennis steadily, like he was genuinely confused about something. "So hang on. If he'd done it before...I don't get...why are you here?"

Dennis stared vacantly into the distance. I guess that's when everything began to fall into place for me. Why Dennis had come on this trip. All of it.

It must have made sense to Dwayne, too. "Wait...so you planned this?" he asked.

Dennis's face tightened for a moment and a darkness filled his eyes. "I wasn't sure the cocksucker was gonna try it again, but if he did it was gonna be the last time..."

Thunder boomed in the distance. The echo seemed to roll on through all eternity. Dwayne stared blankly at Dennis. "You planned this."

Kevin lunged at Dennis. He seized him by the neckline of his T-shirt and screamed full into his face: "You little son of a bitch! You set us up!"

Dennis's feet flew out from under him and they both went down—hard. Dennis's T-shirt came apart in Kevin's hands as they hit the ground and rolled over and over in the muck. Then Kevin was on top, landing blow after blow to the side of

Dennis's head. He got in a good half dozen licks before Dwayne grabbed Kevin by the seat of his pants and pulled him off. They were so covered in mud and leaves and blood it was hard to tell them apart. Or it would have been if Dennis hadn't been such a runt.

"Enough, goddammit!" Dwayne cried. He dropped Kevin into the mud and stood over Dennis like a bodyguard. "Are you *trying* to get us killed?"

Had the hillbillies heard us? We pricked up our ears, listening for sounds inside the walls. A dog barked a few times. A circular saw whined. A radio played an REO Speedwagon tune.

And I'm not missing a thing, watching the full moon crossing the range.

Kevin slowly got to his feet and his eyes flashed with anger. "You fucking psycho! You planned this the whole time!" He turned to me and James and waved a hand toward Dennis. "He's been lying to us this whole time, using us for his sick little revenge scheme. He's nothing but a fucking psychopath—like his uncle!"

Dennis started to move away, then I saw his hand fly to his jeans pocket. He spun and lunged at Kevin. Dwayne must have anticipated it. He was ready. He got hold of Dennis's arm and twisted it behind his back and body-slammed him to the ground, face-first, his knee pressed into his upper back. He pried the pocketknife away from Dennis's grasp and tossed it away into the darkness.

Dwayne kept his knee buried in Dennis's back while his eyes searched for something. He picked up his big, heavy flashlight half-buried in the mud. "Try something like that again and I *will* crack your skull open with this," Dwayne said.

He wasn't joking.

Kevin slowly drew a flat hand across his mouth. He looked like he *really* wanted another crack at Dennis, but he wisely resisted.

We all took a deep breath. For me, it was a big sigh of relief.

Now that Dennis had tried to kill Kevin, now that he had admitted to plotting this whole crazy revenge scheme, Kevin and James would have to agree to go to the sheriff. No way in hell would they go along with Dennis now that we knew this whole trip was a setup.

Dwayne removed his knee from Dennis's back. Dennis slowly got to his knees and picked up Father Ted's muddy Panama hat and put it on. He was quite the sight. His muddy T-shirt hung in tatters and blood oozed from his nose. He got to his feet and brushed some muddy leaves off his jeans and turned away and crawled slowly up the rise back to the rock outcropping, and there he sat on the ledge hunched up and hugging his arms to his chest and glaring down angrily at us.

Dwayne spat on the ground. "So y'all lied to me about it being self-defense too." He drew a long breath and let it out slowly, like he'd just finished a mile run. "If your buddy planned this whole thing like he says...that makes it premeditated. I ain't no big-city lawyer but even I know there ain't no such thing as premeditated self-defense. That's just straight-up murder." He shook his head miserably. "You little bastards got me mixed up in a murder case."

There was a silence, then Kevin said, "We didn't know he planned it."

"Just shut the fuck up," Dwayne snapped. "I don't believe a word you punks say."

It was quiet a moment. Even the radio and the power tools seemed to go silent. Suddenly Dwayne got a pained look on his face and he cried out, "Son of a bitch! Now I am fucked!"

"Why?" James said.

"Why? I'll tell you why! I got them keys for you! I drove you all over the goddamn county. Even if I say I didn't know nothing about a dead priest, that fuckhead sheriff ain't gonna miss a chance to lock me up. He's been waiting years for this."

I wondered what he'd done that made this sheriff so eager to lock him up, but I wasn't about to ask.

"What I ought to do is just leave your asses out here to freeze to death," Dwayne said. "That's the only thing that makes sense." He threw his head back and roared: "FUCK!"

The dogs definitely heard that. All four of them shifted their barking into high gear. I figured we'd beat it the hell out of there now, that'd we head back to the truck as fast as our legs could carry us. We might even stop by the sheriff's office.

Wrong again. Apparently it didn't matter what craziness Dennis did. Kevin and James were still dead-set against going to the cops.

James said, "C-c-can't you just help us get the Jeep so we c-c-can get out of here."

Dwayne stared at him. "There's no way in hell you're gonna get that Jeep."

Kevin said, "We gotta try!"

"Hey, by all means. Don't let me stop you."

"There's only two of them," Kevin said. "Ain't you got any weapons in your pickup? I thought you country people always carried two or three shotguns in your gun rack. Why can't we just march in there with a couple of shotguns and lock them up in a shed and take our Jeep?"

Shotguns? Had they completely lost their minds? Now they were talking about a shootout with a bunch of crazy backwoods car thieves. It was like they were determined to get us all killed. And for what? To protect some psychotic kid we barely even knew?

Dwayne laughed bitterly. "That's some plan! You drive back to St. Louis safe and sound and in a couple weeks some coon hunters will stumble on little bits and pieces of my chopped-up corpse. No thank you."

Somebody yelled at the dogs to shut the hell up. Then the radio was turned up as a familiar Foreigner tune came on. Nobody said anything for a long time. I wasn't sure if Dwayne's offer to drive us back to town still stood, but I sure hoped so. When he headed back to his truck, I planned on being right on his heels.

Only it turned out I was wrong about Dwayne too. He suddenly let out a long breath and said, "For the sake of argument, let's say you got that Jeep back. Then what are you gonna do—now that you know Al Capone up there masterminded this whole revenge scheme? Are you still gonna tell your daddy the cop?"

The rain dripped on the leaves. *Feeling like the first time*, Foreigner sang.

Kevin shook his head. "We drive home and say Father Ted dropped us off at the church and we never saw him again. We ditch the Jeep down by the river. Make it look like he got mixed up in something bad."

A moment ticked by. Dwayne said, "That was your plan all along, wasn't it?"

Kevin half-shrugged.

"What about your friend lying out there in the woods?"

"We buried him," Kevin said.

"Of course you did." Dwayne slowly shook his head. "So I either gotta take my chances with a bunch of lying, murdering delinquents or a fucking sadistic sheriff. That's great. That's just fucking great." He paused for a moment, then he laughed bitterly. "Try to make a little quick cash and next thing you know my dumb ass is mixed up in a murder. Story of my fucking life."

There was a long silence. "So?" Kevin said.

Dwayne let go a heavy sigh. "At least with your stupid plan there's a chance. It's almost zero, but it's a chance." His lips pressed tight in a rigid smile. "Let's go get that Jeep."

CHAPTER 15

DWAYNE'S EYES drifted to the rocky outcropping where Dennis sat huddled like a wounded soldier. "Wait here," Dwayne said, then he turned and started up the slope. He slipped and fell and slid halfway down again, but he got right back up. After three tries and a lot of cursing, he made it to the ledge. He stepped around Dennis and leaned out over the ledge overlooking the chop shop.

"What's he doing?" James said.

"Beats me," Kevin said.

"I hope he ain't asking Dennis's advice," I said.

After a minute Dwayne climbed down. He wiped his muddy hands on the back of his jeans and said, "Here's how this is gonna work…if it works. Which it probably won't."

"That's reassuring," I said.

Dwayne grinned slightly. "You're gonna need a diversion. And when I think diversion, I think fire."

"You do know it's raining?" I said.

Dwayne's eyes landed on me with undisguised annoyance. "Don't interrupt me again." He was serious.

"One of y'alls gonna start a fire on the far side of the lot. Toss a bottle of gasoline through a window or garage door. While them two peckerwoods is trying to put out the fire, another of ya's gonna hightail it over the wall—or under the wall, whichever—and go for the Jeep." He spat out a stream of tobacco juice and looked thoughtful. "If you're lucky the garage door ain't locked."

"And if we ain't lucky?" James said.

Dwayne gave us his cowboy shrug. "Then hopefully your deaths will be quick and relatively painless."

There was an extended silence during which everyone grew colder and wetter and considerably more miserable.

"That's your plan?" James said.

"Genius can be recognized by its childish simplicity," Dwayne said.

"What's that?"

"What? That quote?"

James nodded.

"Something the janitor at my high school used to say. Ol' Lefty Kretchmer." He looked thoughtful. "I reckon he's long dead by now."

I let out a long, exasperated sigh. "We may get a chance to pay our respects real soon."

Dennis had rejoined us. "Say we get the Jeep started, how're we supposed to get it out of there?" he said. "There's a big hunkin' chain across the front gate."

"Bolt cutters. Gotta pair in my toolbox." His face broke into a grin. "What, doesn't everybody?"

Thank God for beer-guzzling, pickup-truck driving, working-class Americans and their toolboxes, I thought to myself for perhaps the first and last time.

"One of y'all will have to cut the lock and to get the gate open," Dwayne said. "Good thing there's four of you."

"What are *you* gonna do?" Kevin said.

"Me? I'm going out to my truck and getting the hell out of here."

The four of us shared a look at this.

"*Don't* worry. I'll fix up the Molotov cocktail before I go, and I'll show you how to use the bolt cutters. But what I ain't

JACKS FORK

gonna do is get my dick shot off for no reason. Besides, you don't need me. As long as everyone does their part. Don't *fuck* up their part, I mean."

I shifted nervously on my feet. It was crazy. His plan would never work. Never in a million years.

"I'm gonna run back to my truck and get the bolt cutters and the flammable liquids," Dwayne said. He turned on the flashlight. "Try not to kill each other while I'm gone." Then he hesitated. "Or go ahead and kill each other. I don't give a shit either way."

I glanced at the others for a moment and when I looked back again Dwayne and his flashlight were gone, sucked into the dense black hole of forest where not even light could escape. "This is nuts," I said. "That guy's gonna get us all k-k-killed."

"Nah, what are they gonna do?" Dennis said. "They can't do nothing to us for taking back our own Jeep."

"How're they gonna know it's ours?" I said. "Besides, we're talking about trespassing, property damage, arson. That's three reasons to shoot us right there. Not that guys like that need a reason."

Dennis waved his hand dismissively. "You worry too much, Doofus," he said, then he peeled off what was left of his T-shirt and wadded it into a ball and tossed it away. The shirt landed with a muddy plop at the foot of the wall. Dennis didn't seem to be affected by the cold at all, which is what you might expect from a freakshow like Dennis. He gave James a nudge. "Tell him, cuz. Everything's gonna be copacetic, ain't it?"

James looked deathly pale as he shoved his hands in his jean's pockets and shivered.

I thought about going after Dwayne, before he got too far ahead. Following him out to the pickup. And once I got to the highway I could start hitchhiking. But once again something held me back. Maybe it was the madness of trying to hitchhike at midnight in the freezing rain in the middle of the Mark Twain National Forest. Maybe I was afraid Dennis and Kevin would come after me. I couldn't take on both of those crazy fuckers. Or maybe it was the thought that if they did succeed in getting the Jeep, they could be on the road in fifteen minutes, more or less, headed home. Without me.

Kevin seemed to have read my thoughts. He studied me for a moment and said, "You don't have to do anything, okay? We don't need your candy ass. All you gotta do is stay out of the way. You can do that, can't you?"

I felt my face grow hot, partly out of anger and partly due to a great jumble of feelings and emotions it would take years to decode. Again I went off by myself. I leaned against a cottonwood, trying to resist the temptation to feel sorry for myself. The cold rain dripped down, splashing on my head. I peeled off my T-shirt and wrung some of the water out of it and slipped it back on. A while later I heard Kevin say, "What's taking him? You think he ran out on us?"

"If he had any brains," I muttered to myself.

Another long slow moment ticked by.

"I don't think he's coming back," Kevin said.

And just like that the rain stopped. I wasn't sure if that was a good thing or what. The others would probably take it for a sign from heaven. A good omen. Then I saw the light bobbing in the distance and I rejoined the others.

It was Dwayne all right. There was a palpable sense of relief in the air.

He had an old green canvas bag slung over one shoulder. "Stopped raining," he said. He tossed Dennis the flashlight and dropped the bag to the ground and squatted beside it. He did a double take at Dennis. "Where's your shirt?"

"Ain't nothing left of it."

He gave Dennis a hard look. "That's a clue, dumbass! We don't want to give these hillbillies any help identifying us. Now go get it."

"It ain't like it's got my name on it."

"Now!"

JACKS FORK

Dennis glared at Dwayne. For a moment I thought we were in for a Mexican standoff. Then Dennis muttered something under his breath and went to fetch his T-shirt. Maybe he wasn't as crazy as we thought.

Dwayne watched him go. Then he shook his head and opened the bag and took out a pair of bolt cutters.

"Who wants these?"

"I'll take 'em," James said.

"You ever use one of these?"

James shook his head.

"Course not," Dwayne said. He gripped the handles and demonstrated the basic bolt-cutting technique. "Now when you get to the gate you're gonna want to find the padlock. Then you're gonna slide the blades on the shackle—"

"The what?" James said.

Dwayne rolled his eyes and sighed heavily. "Fucking city boys," he said. "The U-shaped piece of metal."

"Oh..."

"Now—this is important—you want to hold the bolt cutter waist-high, like so. You take the grips and squeeze the handles hard as you can 'til it bites through. It's gonna take a helluva lot of pressure. You might not get it the first time. Or the second." He handed James the bolt cutters. "Think you got it?"

James nodded, but it wasn't a confident nod.

Dwayne glanced briefly at Dennis who had rejoined our group, his ruined T-shirt slung over his shoulder. "Shine that light over here so I can see what I'm doing," he told Dennis. Then he went into the canvas bag and drew out an empty beer bottle and crammed it down into the mud a little. He took out a gallon gas can and a can of motor oil and a piece of a dingy gray rag, and set these next to the bottle.

From out of the west came the low rumble of distant thunder. We stood around Dwayne in a rough semi-circle, shivering. For a long moment he was silent, his face knotted in thought.

"I can't believe I'm doing this," he said.

"What?" Kevin said.

Dwayne drew a deep breath. "Change of plan. I'm gonna set the fire. I can't trust you knuckleheads with something like this. You'll blow yourselves up, sure as shit."

Nobody argued.

Dwayne stared into space. "I'm too fucking kind-hearted. That's my problem. Mister Fucking Nice Guy. It's gonna be the death of me." He shook his head, then he went back to work. He slipped a finger into the gas can and drew out the plastic nozzle. "I'm not exactly sure about the proportions…We'll do half and half. That oughta have some kind of effect, I would think."

Dwayne filled the bottle and dribbled some oil on the rag and stuffed the rag into the neck of the bottle. He wiped his hands on his jeans, and said, "Now, which two of you are gonna get the Jeep?"

"Me and Dennis will," Kevin said. "I got the keys."

Dennis shifted his feet. "I'd prefer to throw that firebomb."

"I'm sure you would," Dwayne said.

"Why do we need two of us to get the Jeep?" Dennis said.

"'Cause while one of you is getting your ass mauled by them dogs, the other one just might make it to the garage."

I guess that made as much sense as anything else.

Dwayne peered at us for a moment. "Now listen up, as soon as you see smoke, you haul your ass over the fence. Hopefully them peckerwoods will be heading for the fire and the dogs will be right on their heels." He stopped, drew himself up. "Once you get the Jeep started you head straight for the front gate. If it ain't open you're gonna need to bust through it, ya hear? Then you're gonna stop so me and this one"—he nodded at James—"can get in. And I'm getting behind the wheel." He paused a second. "Questions?"

"You ain't said what we do if the garage is locked," Kevin said.

Dwayne laughed grimly. "I don't know about you, but I'm

hauling ass back to my truck and getting the hell out of here."

"What about me?" I said. "What do I do?"

"Assuming everything goes perfectly—which it won't—you're gonna drive my truck." He dug into his pocket and tossed me his keys. "You know how to drive a stick, right?"

"I don't even know how to drive an automatic."

"You've never driven a *vee*hicle before? How old are you?"

"Fifteen."

"You're fifteen and you never drove a car?"

"I drove a riding lawn mower one summer on my grandpa's place, back in—"

Dwayne held up his hand to cut me off. "About as useful as a windshield wiper on a goat's ass." He turned and laid his eyes on James levelly. "How about you? Ever drive a stick?"

"A few times. It wasn't pretty."

Dwayne sighed heavily and jerked his head toward me. "Give this one the bolt cutters. And *you* give him the keys."

I tossed James the keys.

"There goes what's left of my transmission," Dwayne said with a deep sigh of resignation. He turned to James. "Do you got any kind of light so you can find your way back to the highway?"

James shook his head.

"Of course not." He turned to face Dennis. "Give him the flashlight."

Dennis hurled the flashlight at James. James had to dive to catch it.

Dwayne glared at Dennis. Then he turned back to James. "Just sit tight 'til you see us come up the road. Hopefully in the Jeep. As soon as you see our headlights, you head south. The truck's already pointed in that direction. Just take the highway all the way to Route C about a quarter mile, then take that north all the way into town. Meet us in back of The Mule Lip. Got it?"

James nodded. "And if you ain't in the Jeep?"

"Then we'll be coming in fast and on foot, so be ready."

Dwayne handed the gas bottle to Kevin and told him not to drop it, then he scrambled back up the slope to the rocks where he could look out over the compound one last time. He wasn't up there long before he slid back down.

"I'm not seeing any Sikas," he said. "But I did see four real ugly pit bulls." He picked up the canvas bag and slung it over his shoulder and he took the Molotov cocktail from Kevin.

"Boys, the way I see it, about one hundred different things can go wrong, and that's being conservative."

"That's a hell of a pep talk," I said.

"Yeah well, I left my inspirational speech in my other suit." He studied us for a while, then he said, "In conclusion…don't fuck this up."

Then he tramped off into the mist.

CHAPTER 16

"ALL RIGHT, let's do this." Kevin turned his gaze on me and James and said, "Try not to get us killed, okay?"

"That goes double for you," I said.

Kevin turned to Dennis. He was gone. "Where the hell did he—?"

I spied Dennis off down the path whittling on a long sycamore branch. It looked to me like he was carving a spear. I couldn't believe it, the little shit had another pocketknife! The guy was a goddamn walking Army Surplus.

"Goddammit, Dennis, what are you doin' now?" Kevin said.

Dennis ran his thumb along the pointy end of the spear. "Almost finished."

"What is that?"

"If them dogs try to rip my balls off, I'm gonna take a couple of the bastards with me."

"That's great. Can we go now?"

Dennis folded away his pocketknife and got to his feet. "We can now."

James and I watched them head off toward the fence, then we set off down the path toward the front gate.

"A fire sure sounds good, doesn't it?" James said.

I suppose he was trying to be funny, but I wasn't in the mood for jokes. Not even graveyard humor. Anyway, I was still kicking myself for saying I couldn't drive a stick. I could've faked it. Probably. "You're lucky, you know that?" I said. "You'll probably be the only one that makes it out of here alive."

"I just hope I c-c-can remember how to drive a stick," James said. "Where's reverse again?"

"You're asking me?"

"It's either up and left or down and all the way right."

"Well, you gotta fifty-fifty chance."

It was time for me to break off. I told James I'd see him in hell. I thought that would be the cool thing to say, in case they were my last words. Then I cut through some brush until I found the muddy dirt road which I followed to the front gate. Someone had written *Trespasers will be shot and eatin by killer dogs!* on the gate in orange spray paint. Even at death's door, I couldn't help but notice all the grammatical errors.

I stood under the dripping leaves and studied the bolt cutters in my hands. Do I wait until they get the fire going or do I cut the lock now? If I do it now I might draw the attention of the dogs and that could alert the Sikas that something was up and that could ruin everything. But if I waited and I had trouble with the lock...I'd never used bolt cutters before. What if I wasn't able to make the cut? Experience had taught me that nothing was ever easy, especially under pressure. Not even the simplest of tasks. And this was definitely not a simple task.

I probably had a minute or two before the fire got going, so I slipped back into the trees and tried the bolt cutters out on some pine branches. I went to work on some of the lower limbs, snipping off bits of branches and twigs until I figured I was ready for the real thing. Then I found a spot where it was pitch-dark and hunkered down and waited for the fire to start.

The hounds must have sensed something was wrong because they got all riled up, racing along the fence, nipping at each other's hind legs and yapping their fool heads off. Somebody told the dogs to hush, but they kept right at it.

Then things began to happen. Angry voices rose above the whirr of the diesel generators and the bay of the dogs. Cautiously I crept over to the fence and peered through one of the cracks in the gate. A deep orange glow shimmered between two metal buildings. One of the Sikas hauled ass around the side of the building, carrying one of those big handheld fire extinguishers. Two pit bulls were at his heels, snapping at each other as they ran.

I glanced around for Dennis and Kevin and spotted them just as Kevin dropped over the fence, landing hard on all fours. He sprinted low across the open yard toward the garage. Dennis followed, bare-chested and carrying that stupid spear and looking like a wild man. Father Ted's hat blew off his head and Dennis turned and went back for it. *Unbelievable.* He grabbed the hat and followed Kevin's tracks across the yard.

Then they were at the garage door.

I couldn't believe my eyes. Dwayne's plan was going like clockwork.

And then it wasn't. Kevin couldn't get the garage door up. Dennis gave it a try, but he wasn't having any luck either. He tried to pry the door open with his spear and the spear snapped in half.

I don't know what happened after that because I had to get to work on the padlock. However it turned out, I was *not* going to get the blame for blowing the mission.

The mission. Like we were Navy SEALs or some shit.

The lock, of course, was brand-spanking-new, a real heavy-duty brass Master Lock. Probably the only new thing on the premises. I couldn't see how the flimsy-looking bolt cutters were going to have any effect on it, but I locked the blades on the shackle like Dwayne showed us and gave it everything I had.

It didn't do much. I tried again, this time really throwing my weight behind it. And this time the blades slipped off the shackle and I got a nice long slice across my knuckles. It stung like a son of a bitch. But it didn't look too terrible. I wasn't going to bleed out or anything.

More cursing and barking and yelling from the back of the lot. I peered through the gate into the smoky compound. For the first time since we'd left home, my heart leapt with something like joy. The garage door was wide open.

I still hadn't heard an engine start up, though. Maybe they'd already started dismantling the engine.

I shook off the thought. *The lock. Focus.*

This time I tried to work some leverage by bracing one of the handles against the gate and pushing on the other with both arms. But there was too much give in the gate for that to work. I cursed myself. I had one lousy task and I couldn't even do that.

Where the hell was Dwayne? I glanced around in a near panic. That blaze must have been an inferno by now, judging from all the smoke and noise and chaos. Dwayne could probably cut the lock in a heartbeat. What the hell was keeping him?

A small explosion echoed through the forest, like a firecracker going off in an empty dumpster. I nearly leapt out of my skin. Suddenly I was nose-down on the ground, half-buried in the muddy ruts of monster truck tires. A second blast followed. I scrambled on my hands and knees until I reached the safety of a vine-covered, weed-hidden rusted vehicle of some sort. Whatever it was, it sure beat hiding behind a pine tree.

I couldn't tell where the blasts were coming from, or even if I was the target. I held my breath and huddled against the abandoned vehicle. I didn't hear any more blasts, but inside the fence things were pure bedlam. Somewhere an engine turned over. The Jeep? The monster truck? Or one of a hundred other cars? Either way, I was out of time. I got to my feet and I reeled back to the gate. I took a cursory glance at the lock. I'd made some progress; there were divots in the shackle where the blades had bit into it. Not much, but something. I lined up the blades with the deepest cut and gave it everything I had.

GAAAAAAAAAH!

It still wasn't enough.

Where the fuck was Dwayne?

A vehicle was approaching fast. I couldn't see it, but I heard it come to a stop in front of the gate. A car door opened.

"What the fuck, Doofus? Why isn't this gate open?" Kevin's voice, somewhere on the spectrum between pissed and panicked. "You had one fucking job to do!"

I wasn't really listening to him though. I leaned on the bolt cutters, again using the gate for leverage. Then something slipped or snapped and my hand smashed into the gate. I sank to my knees as the pain shot up my arm and exploded out the top of my head. It felt like I'd broken every bone in my hand. I let out some kind of distressed animal cry, the sound a water buffalo would make as a lion sinks its jaws into its neckbones.

"Did you get it?" Kevin said.

I was in too much pain and too angry to respond. Already my hand was leaking blood like a busted spigot. I got to my feet and studied the padlock. Part of the shackle was gone. With my good hand, I knocked off the lock and swung the gate open.

Kevin grabbed my arm and drew me toward the Jeep. "Get in, they're right behind us!" He hurriedly glanced around. "Where the hell's your friend?"

Dwayne. He was still missing in action. "He ain't here." I scrambled around to the passenger side and climbed into the back seat and dumped the bolt cutters on the floorboards. Dennis was up front, riding shotgun.

"Were those gunshots?" he said.

"What the fuck you think?" Kevin said, sliding behind the wheel.

"They're shooting at us?"

Nobody said anything.

"Well, we can't wait," Kevin said. "It's every man for himself."

I glanced out the window hoping to see Dwayne sprinting around the corner of the fence, but there was nothing out there but darkness. One of those one hundred things that might have gone wrong must have gone wrong. Maybe several of them. I knew I should say something, like, "Guys, we can't leave him." But I didn't. I didn't say a goddamn thing.

Dennis stuck his head out the window and looked back. "Here they come!"

The monster truck's engine turned over. The truck's off-road lights lit up the entire compound. Then the truck lurched forward, throwing up breakers of mud. At the same time one of the Sikas came charging around the corner of the garage on foot. In one hand he carried a double-barreled shotgun. I saw him slip in the mud and go down and there was a flash as the gun went off.

The Jeep's wheels bit into the mud, caught, and we spun through the gate.

"Wait!"

The cry came from somewhere outside the fence. I squinted out the side window into the darkness. Dwayne was about fifty feet from the Jeep, limping badly. He was having a hard time getting to us.

"I see him!" I cried.

The monster truck was closing in. At that moment my mind flashed on the image of the truck rolling up a ramp, going airborne and flattening our Jeep like a pancake.

What a stupid way to die that would be.

Kevin called out the window. "Move your ass!"

I threw open the back door and Dwayne pitched in beside me. He smelled of smoke and raw alcohol sweat.

"Go, go, go!" he cried.

Kevin hit the gas. The tires spun in the ruts. Spun and spun. The Jeep had zero traction. The tires sank deeper and deeper into the muck. I had one thought. *Really, we get this far and we get stuck in the fucking mud!*

Don't ask me how, but one of the tires caught and we lurched ahead. All of the sudden we were moving forward through the trees. I glanced behind us just as there was another muzzle flash followed shortly by a blast and the *ping, ping, ping* of shot hitting the back of the Jeep. Any higher and it would have taken out the back window.

Kevin hit the brights and the trees lit up.

Dwayne tossed his backpack onto the floor. "A fucking twelve-gauge," he muttered. "Right in the fucking thigh."

I put my head down on the seat and stayed down. We seemed to be moving sideways as much as we moved forward. I remember making one of those deals of desperation with the Lord: *You save my dumb ass and I'll go to Mass every morning until I die.* Something like that.

Then we were on blacktop and I told the Lord I had to go, but I'd get back to him.

Kevin pointed the Jeep's nose north toward town.

"You're gonna have to go faster than this," Dwayne said.

I peered over the front seat. The speedometer was right at fifty-five.

"It's too slick," Kevin cried.

Not only that, but the roads were all twisted, too, snaking up and down foothills skirting 600-foot dropoffs. Kevin kicked it up to sixty, his knuckles whitening on the steering wheel. I glanced over at Dwayne. He looked like his pain was at a ten. He'd pulled down his jeans and jammed a finger into a jagged hole in his leg the size of a baseball. Then he stripped off his T-shirt and pressed it into the wound with both hands while blood oozed through his fingers. A lot of it.

I choked down a dry heave. For a moment, I forgot all about my busted hand. "How bad is it?" I said.

Dwayne gritted his teeth. "Hurts worse than it looks," he said. Then, "I didn't think the bastards would bring a shotgun to a fire. Who the hell does that?"

"I'm pretty sure you need a doctor," I said.

He shook his head. "The fucker that shot me's probably sitting in the lobby of the emergency room right now waiting to

ID me." His face tightened with pain and he looked out the back window. There was only endless darkness behind us.

"But—"

"No detours," he said. "We stick to the plan. It's worked so far. For you lucky sonsabitches, anyway."

CHAPTER 17

WE WEREN'T OUT of the woods yet—both literally *and* figuratively. The rain had started up again, though it wasn't much more than a drizzle. We'd gone less than a mile when a pair of super-high-power flood lights blazed up in the rear window.

"We got company," Dennis cried.

"Damnit, that was my favorite shirt," Dwayne said between clenched teeth. He'd torn his T-shirt in half and tied it around his upper thigh. "Got it at the Queen concert in St. Louis...last February." He glanced up at Kevin and said, "You might want to step it up there, bud."

Behind us, the flood lights grew brighter. There were a lot of them. Like a jetliner coming in for a landing. The monster truck obviously had a lot more engine than the crappy little one in the Jeep Wagoneer.

"If I go any faster we're gonna end up at the bottom of one of these hills," Kevin said.

"If you don't we're gonna end up there anyways," Dwayne said.

I'd been studying the road signs along the way. They all said the same thing, either WINDING ROAD AHEAD or SLIPPERY WHEN WET. Meanwhile our pursuers had neared to within a hundred feet and were closing rapidly.

A few seconds later they were right up on our ass, and the inside of the Jeep lit up like high noon. We rocked forward as the truck slammed into our back bumper.

"Son of a bitch!" cried Kevin. "What the fuck?"

"He's trying to push us off the road!" Dennis said.

"Put the light on," Dwayne said.

"What?" I said.

"The dome light!"

I wasn't sure why he needed more light—the flood lights were putting out plenty—but I did what he asked. Dwayne went into his canvas bag and drew out a wine bottle. *What a time to start drinking,* I thought.

The truck slammed us again. Our backend fishtailed and struck a guard rail. The noise sounded like a buzzsaw cutting through an anchor.

"GODDAMN IT!" Dwayne cried. "Can't you go any faster!"

"No, I can't!" Kevin shouted.

Dwayne wedged the wine bottle between his thighs and he picked up the can of gasoline. He called out: "I need a funnel. Find something...some paper...anything."

"What are you gonna do?" I said.

"I'm gonna fry that sumbitch."

Dennis rooted through the glove box and handed Dwayne an old road map. Dwayne made a half-assed funnel with the map and poured some gasoline into the bottle, but mostly he spilled the gas on his shot-up leg. He seized up and his face tightened in pain as though his brain had caught fire. I've never seen anyone in that much pain before or since.

We slowed for a hairpin curve and the crazy son of a bitch slammed us again. The Jeep fishtailed first right, then left.

Well, this is it, I thought. Any second now we'll plunge off the far side of the highway down a six-hundred-foot ravine and flip end over end to the jagged rocks below and burst into flame like some bad 1970s Hollywood movie ending.

But somehow Kevin managed to regain control. Talk about beginner's luck. It was the second time that trip that I was grateful Kevin Przybysz was with us.

Dwayne dug into the canvas bag and drew out the can of motor oil and splashed some of it into the funnel. "I need somebody's sock." He looked at me. "You. Gimme your sock."

"Which one?" I said.

"I don't...the driest one!"

"They're both wet."

"Give!"

I kicked off my tennis shoe and peeled off one of my sweat socks. It wasn't as damp as I thought it would be.

"A knife," Dwayne said. He glanced up into Dennis's face. "Hey you! Killer! Gimme your knife, now!"

Dennis dug into his pocket and passed a jackknife over the seat. "That's my last one," he said.

"Good!" Dwayne said. He hacked the sock into strips and used a piece of sock to sop up some of the spilled oil and gasoline from his jeans and stuffed it into the bottle. He held out the bottle to me. "You're gonna have to do this. I can't."

The monster truck was riding our bumper again, pushing us all over the road, from one lane to the other. I stared blankly at the bottle in Dwayne's hand, not quite grasping what he was asking of me.

"Once you light it, aim for the windshield," he said. "You got it?"

"What? I can't—"

He handed me the bottle. "We ain't got time to debate this. Do it!"

I took hold of the bottle with my one good hand, which definitely was not my throwing hand.

"Take the lighter," he said. "And keep that flame away from me. I'm soaked in gasoline."

We rocked forward again, violently. The Jeep's front bumper screeched along a guard rail, letting off a fountain of sparks, a few landing in the back seat. Dwayne's eyes nearly popped out of his head.

Kevin got us straightened out again.

"Now!" Dwayne screamed into my face.

"I can't!" I whimpered. "My hand's...I—I can't throw—"

"Jesus titty-fucking Christ!" Dwayne cried. "What are you waiting for?"

"Give it to me!" Dennis said. He leaned over the front seat and yanked the bottle out of my hand. He ran down his window and flicked his Bic lighter. The sock went up like a Roman candle. I can see it still, blazing in his hand as he leaned out the window, bare chested, waving that flaming bottle. He let out some kind of Indian war whoop. I waited for the truck to slam into us and for Dennis to topple out the window. That's what I expected to happen.

Then Dennis reared back and let the bottle go.

A massive fireball erupted across the truck's windshield. The driver slammed the brakes and the truck spun ninety degrees and struck a guardrail. We rounded a sharp curve and I lost sight of it. All I could see in the rear window was a dull flickering glow that grew more and more dim as we sped on.

Dennis danced in the open window, pounding the top of the roof with both hands and laughing maniacally. "Did you see that? A fuckin' bull's-eye!" He ducked back into the Jeep and turned to look at me and Dwayne, a big shit-eating grin on his face. "That was so freaking cool!"

"Is he still behind us?" Dwayne said.

We turned to look. "Fuck no," Dennis cried. "Ain't nobody coming. He's probably at the bottom of the mountain by now." His smile widened and his gaze shifted to Dwayne. "Hey man, you got another one of them bottles?"

Dwayne sunk back into his seat and let out a long breath.

For the first time I felt something other than contempt for Dennis, Kevin and Dwayne. For one, brief moment, I was glad we were on the same side.

JACKS FORK

Kevin slowed the Jeep to forty-five, then forty. Dennis was still hopping around excitedly in the passenger side like he had a winning lottery ticket. "You gotta show me how to make them things," he told Dwayne.

Once things calmed down, I began to feel stupid, ashamed even. They didn't know about my busted hand; they probably thought I had chickened out. Maybe I had. Maybe I could have thrown with a busted-up hand, though knowing my aim I would have missed the truck by quarter mile.

Anyway, it was all for the best. And unlike Dennis, I was glad I hadn't killed anyone. Even if the bastard deserved it.

Surprisingly, nobody ragged me about being a coward. Not even Kevin.

I cradled my injured hand and slumped against the door and stared out the window at the passing darkness. I had no idea where we were, just lost in some foggy, endless stretch of foothills. I glanced sidelong at Dwayne. The poor guy was barechested and covered in sweat and his face looked white as a bleached blanket.

I said, "We need to get you to the hospital." I was thinking about myself, too. Maybe someone could take a look at my hand while we were there.

"Not gonna happen," Dwayne said. "They know they hit me. The ER is the first place they'll look." Dwayne looked like his brain was on fire. "It didn't hit the bone. I'll be all right in a couple of days. Long as it don't get infected bad."

"Does it hurt much?" Kevin said.

"Ever been bit by a hornet?"

"U- huh."

"Well, it's like that, only multiply it by ten thousand."

I said, "Couldn't we take you to an ER in a different county?"

Dwayne shook his head. "If I know them crazy sonsabitches, they'll check every ER in southern Missourah 'til they find somebody with a load of buckshot in his ass."

After that it got real quiet in the Jeep, nothing but the sound of wipers slapping back and forth. A pickup, its bed loaded with wet caged chickens, passed us heading south. Nobody said anything for a while, then Kevin wondered aloud if we thought we'd killed whoever was in the monster truck.

"We could go back and check," Dennis said. "I'd kinda like to see where they ended up."

"Keep driving," Dwayne said. "The sooner your dumb asses are out of Iron County, the better."

WE WERE ON the road for another ten minutes, with Dwayne giving halting directions through gritted teeth. Dennis came up with a pint of Smirnoff from under the seat ("Here's that vodka we owe you") and Dwayne splashed some in the open wound (after which he screamed and nearly kicked the door off the Jeep) and guzzled the rest like they do in old Western movies. I could have stood some vodka, too, but I didn't dare ask. I studied my hand in the dark and wondered how bad it was…if I'd ever throw a baseball or strum a guitar again. Dennis dialed the radio to 1120 AM, hoping to get the Cardinals game, like it was just another Friday night cruising around the city, but Kevin made him turn it off so he could concentrate. When we pulled into Iron Mountain, downtown was dark and quiet and Main Street was even deader than before. A single motorcycle leaned in front of The Mule Lip. We drove around to the rear of the building, where Dwayne's blue pickup idled in the gravel lot. James sat behind the wheel, looking about as relieved as a fifteen-year-old girl with a negative pregnancy test.

We drew up alongside the pickup.

"My God!" James cried. "I can't believe you did it!" His whole face broke into a grin. "That's freaking unbelievable. I thought for sure I'd seen the last of you guys." Then he must have got a good look at Dwayne and his grin faded. "Anybody hurt?"

We waited for Dwayne to say something, but he remained stoically silent. And I sure wasn't going to whine about my busted hand.

"Sounds like a no," James said. "Anybody follow you?"

"Briefly," Dennis said.

"We'll tell you all about it on the way home," Kevin said.

"Hell yeah," James said. "How soon do we start?"

Dwayne leaned his head out the window. "How's my transmission?"

James shifted uneasily.

"Well?"

"Actually...you were probably due for a new one anyway," he said.

Dwayne shook his head sadly. I might have felt sorry for him if I hadn't been preoccupied with my own innumerable problems.

Dwayne opened the rear door and drew a long breath and swung his bad leg with the T-shirt tied around it and set it down gingerly on the asphalt. Then he tightened his grip on the door handle and gazed toward the bar. "Hope Doreen put my beer on ice," he said. Then he slid off the edge of the seat and drew himself up on his good leg, then he slowly, carefully hopped over to his pickup. He leaned on the open door while he caught his breath. After a few minutes of sucking air, he said, "This is far from over. You remember what I said when we started all this foolishness?"

Pool balls clicked in the distance and muffled music from a jukebox carried across the mostly empty parking lot. I wasn't sure what he meant. He'd said a lot of things. I hadn't known there'd be a quiz later.

"What I'm saying is...them Sikas, and there's a lot of 'em...they ain't the forgive-and-forget type. Especially if the one in that truck didn't make it." He paused and stared out over the parking lot. His eyes were somber and grave, but on his lips a grin began to widen. "That fire was a lot bigger than I thought it would be. Probably burned down their entire enterprise by now." The smile disappeared. "They're gonna come after us. All of us. And them bastards are like bloodhounds. They're relentless 'til they get what they want."

We were silent, each lost in his own horrible imaginings.

Dwayne reached into his truck and took a fresh tin of Copenhagen off the dash. He thumped it a few times, getting it packed nice and tight.

"How are they gonna know it was us?" James asked.

Dwayne laughed as if he had said something absurdly funny. "For one thing, they got your license plates."

"You mean they saw them?" Kevin said.

"No. I mean they *got* 'em."

I went around to the back of the Jeep. Sure enough, the plates were gone.

"But this Jeep don't belong to us," Kevin said. "It belongs to some old guy from our parish."

Dwayne shook his head. "So you lied to me about that too. I ain't surprised." He hesitated. "In that case you might wanna tell the sorry sumbitch that he should expect a visit from a couple of cold-blooded, sadistic car thieves."

I swallowed hard thinking about that, about what could happen to Mr. Franklin and his wife and his daughters. To Mary Beth.

"We can't really tell anyone about this," Dennis said.

"Yeah, I figured you'd say that." Dwayne leaned against the doorframe of the pickup and put a fresh dip in. "Gonna be all kinds of news coverage about a missing priest who was driving this very same *vee*hicle. You got one thing going for you, though. Y'all are minors so your names might not be in the papers. That might buy you a few more days before the Sikas track you down." Dwayne winced in pain again. "Didn't you say there was some gin, too, or was that a lie too?"

I expected Dennis to object, but I don't think he wasn't even listening. Or maybe he'd had his fill of booze for the day. I hoped so. Lord knows he was crazy enough without it. I dug around under the passenger seat until I found the pint of Beefeater, which I gladly handed over to Dwayne. He studied the label for a moment and cracked the cap and took a long pull off the bottle. Then he let out a long breath. "You probably thought this was over when you planted that preacher."

"I didn't," I said.

Dwayne studied me for a moment. He wiped his mouth with the back of his hand. "Probably thought one of ya going to jail for killing a pervert was the worst that could happen." He screwed the cap back on the gin and tossed it onto the seat beside him. "Don't worry, if them bastards get to me first, I won't give you up. Least not 'til they start sawing off my nuts with a chainsaw."

Dwayne carefully lowered himself to the driver's seat.

"Then again, that might feel good compared to this," he said.

He sat stiffly for a moment waiting for the waves of pain to recede, then he delicately drew up his shot-up leg and lowered his boot gently to the floorboard, cursing under his breath and sputtering the whole time. Then he reached behind the seat and drew out a gray sweatshirt. He pulled on the sweatshirt and said, "I believe you boys owe me something."

We all looked at Dennis. He scowled and reached into his pocket and drew out a wad of bills. He peeled off a twenty and two fives. He hesitated for a second, then he handed the bills to Dwayne.

"Got enough left to get you home?" Dwayne said, tossing the cash onto the dashboard.

"What do you care?" Dennis said scornfully.

"Further away from me the better."

"If we don't, we can always siphon."

"Need a hose for that. There's an old one in my truck bed. Take it. No charge."

Dennis fetched the garden hose out of the truck bed and

tossed it into the back of the Jeep. While he was back there he got a new T-shirt out of his duffel and slipped it on.

At that moment a gaunt, shadowy figure stepped out of the backdoor of The Mule Lip. He staggered a bit, leaned an arm on a railing for balance, and took a long steamy piss against the side of the building. He gave us a cursory glance and went back inside.

"God damn, I thought that sumbitch'd never finish," Dwayne said. He looked about the parking lot and I saw a worried look come into his eye. "We best get before somebody else sees us." He slammed the truck door and picked up the pint of gin and took a hit off the bottle. Then he drew in a long breath and said, "Next time you want to go canoeing, try Crawford County. Got better rivers down there anyway."

He slammed the truck door and started up the truck and shifted into first. The gears ground loud. He winced, either from the pain or the sound of the gears, or maybe it was both, and then he was gone.

CHAPTER 18

KEVIN TOOK IT SLOW and easy as we passed through northern Iron County, keeping well below the speed limit while trying to conserve gas. A nervousness sat in my stomach as I studied the fuel gauge. The needle was flat on E, and there was no sign of a service station, and even if we found one, chances were that it would be closed this time of night. Dennis tried to reassure us in his typical non-reassuring way. If worse came to worse, he could steal around the countryside until he found a pickup or a tractor and siphon its gas. He said we could do it the whole way home if necessary.

Just like we could hotwire the Jeep.

A wretched, gut-wrenching ten minutes passed before a Texaco sign peeked over a ridge off Highway 21 near Pilot Knob. That red-and-green gas station sign was one of the most beautiful sights I'd ever seen.

"You think it's open?" James said.

Nobody said anything. We didn't want to jinx it. I strained my eyes trying to make out signs of life at the station. I saw a few dim lights, but no cars...Check that, there was one car, parked way off to the side.

An employee's car maybe.

In the window, an OPEN sign. A wonderful red, neon, lit-up OPEN sign.

We cheered and pounded on the back of the seats and the dashboard and on each other and let go of two days of pent-up anxiety. We even hugged each other—a big, stinking group hug.

We coasted into the Texaco with a few petrol fumes to spare.

As soon as we drew up to the pumps, Kevin hopped out and put nine dollars of regular in the tank, while Dennis went inside to pay.

James and I got out to stretch our legs. "Think that'll get us home?" I said.

Kevin shrugged his shoulders. "If not, Dennis has got his hose."

Dennis and his goddamn hose. All we needed was to get busted for siphoning gasoline in the parking lot of a Walmart in Festus, Missouri or some other jerkwater town. Then the local cops calling my folks. And our whole stupid plan unraveling like a cheap sweater.

Then again, that might be the best thing that could happen. I still wasn't sure.

We pooled the last of our cash and Kevin went inside and bought a Coke to share and two shriveled hot dogs that we tore in half. We sat in the Jeep and wolfed down the hot dogs like we hadn't eaten in a month. After that, we parked under a vapor light and Kevin spread the oil-stained map of Missouri across the hood and we studied it carefully. Taking 221 north which would get us out of the county the quickest. Then we could head north to Farmington and take 32 north until we got to the Interstate.

It was almost midnight, but with trace amounts of adrenaline still cursing through our veins, none of us was particularly tired.

We pulled back on the highway and followed the winding two-lane north. Dennis messed with the radio until he found a station out of Nashville, Tennessee. WSM, "Home of the Grand Ole Opry," and we listened to that awhile. Mel Tillis sang "Good Woman Blues." Then Eddie Rabbitt came on and did one called "We Can't Go On Living Like This." Eddie Rabbitt's voice seemed to put us all in a better mood. He had a way of doing that. Soon Dennis was sawing logs. Kevin turned down the radio. We drove until we came upon a rest area across the county line and we pulled in there for the night.

A dozen tractor-trailers idled in the rest area's parking lot, spewing thick clouds of diesel smoke. Beside the lot stood a faux-rustic building with restrooms and one of those bronze historical markers. I went inside to take a piss, and on the way back I stopped to read the marker. It said that not far from there at "a small place, of no account," Jesse James and the James-Younger Gang pulled off the first train robbery in Missouri in January 1874. They made off with $12,000, which was a lot of money in those days. Nobody was killed.

I guess that was a big deal in 1874, but to me it was much ado about nothing. Our own much younger band of desperados had killed a priest and at least one shotgun-wielding car thief, and we weren't out of the woods yet. Would our reign of terror be memorialized on an historical marker next to some lonely southern Missouri shit shack a hundred years from now?

I doubted it.

Kevin had crawled into the cargo area and was stretched out in his sleeping bag.

"Are we allowed to sleep here?" I asked.

"It's a rest area, ain't it?"

"Rest area, not sleep area," I said. "What if a state trooper comes by and sees us sleeping in our car?"

Kevin sighed. "So we tell him we're resting, not sleeping. Jesus Christ, you're a doofus."

Did I clobber him? Of course not. I grabbed my sleeping bag and went and curled up in the back seat next to James.

Only I couldn't sleep. Every time a vehicle pulled into the rest area I went into full-on panic mode. James and Kevin couldn't sleep either. Only the guy who had killed two people could sleep. Slept like a baby.

"Maybe we should go over our story one more time," James said.

"Might as well," Kevin said.

"What about Dennis? Should we wake him up?"

Kevin thought about that. "Naw, I prefer him when he's passed out."

James and I nodded in agreement.

James said, "So what are we gonna say about the Jeep, the mangled bumper and bullet holes?"

"Those ain't bullet holes, that's buckshot," Kevin said.

"Whatever. What if the police come around asking about it? What do we say?"

Kevin rose up on one arm. "Simple, we say it must have happened after Father Ted dropped us off. We don't know nothing about it."

I couldn't see James's expression in the dark, but I doubt he was satisfied with that answer. I sure as hell wasn't.

Kevin tried to reassure us. "Look, we don't have to know what happened to the Jeep. All we know is it didn't have a scratch on it when he dropped us off. I'm gonna ditch it in some abandoned lot, some place with a lot of weeds and junk so it'll look like Father Ted got messed up with some bad people after he dropped us off."

"I don't know," I said. "That doesn't seem very likely."

"Seriously? Does anything we've been through the past two days seem likely to you?" He paused, studying our faces. "Well? Does it?"

"No, but—"

"Besides, once they start digging into his personal shit who knows what they're gonna find? You said his room was full of smut, didn't you?"

James nodded.

"Probably full of drugs too," Kevin said. "Who knows, kids might start coming forward, telling what he done to them. Dennis can't be the only one."

James said, "Do we tell the cops about the liquor and the porn?"

Kevin thought about that. "No. Better not. As far as we know, Father Ted was a good guy."

I picked the bolt cutters up off the floorboard. "What about these? Do we get rid of them?"

"No, leave 'em. It'll confuse the cops. The more confused they are the better." Kevin lay down again. "Now let's get some sleep."

I couldn't sleep though. As tired as I was. Every time a car pulled into the rest stop, every time a headlight lit up our windows I was sure it was a state trooper or, worse, the Sikas, and that they had tracked us down and any minute they were going to riddle our Jeep with bullets. It's hard to sleep when you expect to be riddled with bullets at any moment.

The sun was just coming up when I finally nodded off.

CHAPTER 19

WE WERE AWAKENED by the rumble and hiss of a dozen tractor-trailers pulling out of the rest stop. After some quick-and-dirty washing in the foul-smelling restroom, we were back on the road. It was six thirty, still too early to go home—we figured ten or eleven o'clock would be the ideal time to arrive in St. Louis—so we drove around until we found a small city park and loitered on the picnic tables until we began to grow paranoid. What if someone remembered seeing us in the park without Father Ted (*Yes, officer, there were four fifteen-year-old strangers loitering in the park that morning like a bunch of bums...No, there wasn't a priest or an adult of any kind with them, I'm sure about that*). So we piled back into the Jeep and drove around aimlessly, killing time. Eventually we saw a sign for Robinson's Mill State Park. It seemed like there were state parks over every other hill in that part of the country. I guess if the land was too rocky and hilly for farming, it was logged or mined or designated a state park. We followed the signs to Robinson's Mill, then we parked and hiked down a walking trail to a clear narrow river. We didn't know if this river was Jacks Fork or the Black River or the Current River. Or it might have been the St. Francois River. But it didn't matter since we wouldn't be telling anyone that we'd stopped here.

The water was cold as polar ice, way too cold to wade in

that early in the morning, so we sat around on the gravel beach and skipped stones. (Dennis took the gold medal with six skips to James's five. Me, I wasn't much in the mood for games.) Later the talk grew serious. James spoke about how everything was going to be different from now on, how you don't come away from something like this the same way you went in. Dennis, unsurprisingly, said James was full of shit. He said he didn't feel any different. He said he didn't feel anything at all, which is what you would expect a psychopath to say.

Speaking of psychopaths, I asked the others if they believed Dwayne when he said the Sikas wouldn't stop hunting us until they'd tracked us down like hounds after a fox. Kevin said he was probably exaggerating—emphasis on *probably*. We discussed whether we should warn the Franklins, or at least get word to Mr. Franklin that some revenge-seeking hillbilly sociopaths might show up on his doorstep one evening. If anything happened to the Franklins it would be all our fault, and how could we live with ourselves knowing we hadn't even tried to warn them? James and I were for sending Mr. Franklin an anonymous note warning him about the possible danger. Kevin and Dennis were dead-set against it. They said it would be obvious the note was from us, that it would be the same as admitting we'd killed Father Ted. They wouldn't budge on it. Dennis tried to get us to take a blood oath promising that we'd never tell anyone what happened, not even on our deathbeds. He wanted the four of us to slice our palms with his pocketknife (the little shit had *another* pocketknife!) and shake on it.

"No way," I said. "You just want a chance to spill more blood."

"Don't be such a puss," Dennis said.

"Forget it," I said. "With my luck it'll get infected and they'll have to amputate my whole arm." I wasn't a puss. I just didn't want any more stupid, unlucky things (like tetanus or blood poisoning) to happen to me on this trip. Not when the end of this nightmare was nearly in sight.

Kevin told Dennis to drop it and the idea of a blood oath was scrapped.

After that, we each went our separate ways for a while, not so much exploring as just getting off by ourselves. We were sick of each other and desperately needed some alone time. I wandered downstream studying the shallows for bluegill and sunfish and for the big snapping turtles that sunned themselves on half-submerged logs until a strange feeling overtook me. A feeling of intense paranoia, I guess you could say. I was suddenly afraid that the others had driven off without me, leaving me behind to get lost in the woods and die of hunger or drowning or exposure.

One less snitch to worry about.

I hurried back and, yes, I was being paranoid. Kevin was lying on the bank with his arms behind his head staring up at the cloudless steel blue sky. I didn't see James, but Dennis had climbed the bluffs on the far side of the river and sat out on a ledge in his briefs tossing stones and humming a few bars of "Mellow Yellow." After a few minutes of that, Kevin lost it.

"Will you stop with that goddamn song already! Jesus, you're gettin' on my last nerve!"

"Touchy," Dennis said. He tossed a final stone into the river and got to his feet and did a cannonball into the ice-cold current. He stayed under a freakishly long time. I was beginning to get my hopes up that he'd struck a submerged rock and cracked his head open, when he broke the surface and gasped for air like a CIA torture victim.

Then he gave us his big old goofy grin.

Soon James wandered back and the four of us regrouped near the trail's end. As we sat around knocking gravel out of our shoes, Kevin glanced at his watch and said he guessed we'd killed enough time. Dennis slipped into his jeans and T-shirt and glanced about sheepishly. He seemed uneasy about something. Like he wanted to get something off his chest but he wasn't sure how to begin. James and I stood around shuffling our feet nervously, waiting for him to say whatever it was he needed to say.

I just hoped it wasn't another murder confession.

A moment passed. Then Dennis cleared his throat and said, "I, uh...I never thanked you guys for what you did. Not turning me in, I mean. I know we could've all got killed last night, and this shit ain't over yet, but..."

We waited for whatever came after the "but." For a long moment, nothing did. Then he added, "Anyway, I wanted you to know I appreciate it."

I don't know what the others were thinking, but I wanted to tell him to shove it up his ass. That the three of us had been nothing but pawns in his psycho revenge scheme. But I didn't. Maybe because part of me could still see myself turning him in, turning us all in, at some point. Once the peer pressure was off.

James said, "You'd have done the same for us."

"Yeah, maybe," Dennis said, and laughed his kooky-ass laugh. "Hell you guys hardly even know me." He turned to James, standing beside him. "You're my cousin and you hardly know me."

James shrugged. "It could have been any of us," he said, but without much feeling.

Was that true? I wasn't so sure. Getting molested by a priest...repeatedly. I couldn't see it. I could see it happening to James, maybe, if I had to pick one of us.

I don't know. Maybe Dennis couldn't see it happening either—until it happened.

Kevin got to his feet and brushed some gravel from the seat of his pants. "What do you say we get the hell out of this godforsaken place?"

"I thought you'd never ask," James said.

I was way ahead of them.

IT WAS GOING on eight thirty in the morning when we piled

back into the Jeep for the last leg of the drive home. We updated Dennis about what we'd tell our parents—and the police, if need be—once the inquisition started. That the thing to do was to keep our stories simple. The simpler the better. That all we knew was Father Ted dropped us off near our homes around ten o'clock and we said thanks and goodbye and that was it. He didn't say a word about what he planned to do afterward. Nor had he been acting strange or anything. Just his normal self. If they asked what Father Ted talked about on the way home we'd say none of us talked a whole hell of a lot because we were tired and sunburnt and we were listening to the radio (K-SHE, once we could get its signal), but when we did talk it was mostly about baseball, about the Cardinals and who their best starters were (Bob Forsch, John Denny, Pete Vuckovich in that order) and the best hitters (Ted Simmons, Keith Hernandez, Lou Brock, Garry Templeton). And no, there were no dents or bullet holes in the Jeep, at least none that we noticed. Basically we were to say as little as possible. James wasn't a baseball fan; he didn't know the first thing about the Cardinals, so he would say he slept most of the ride home, that he was still feeling poorly. Heat exhaustion, or what have you. If they asked anything else, say you don't remember.

We saw only one patrol car on the way home, sitting in the median between the north and southbound lanes. Somehow he failed to notice our missing license plates and the diminutive size of our driver. We watched the rearview mirror for a good five minutes, but he never did come after us. I think we were more scared of that state trooper than we'd been of that crazy hillbilly in the monster truck who'd tried to run us off the side of a mountain the night before.

As we entered St. Louis County, Kevin made Dennis hand over Father Ted's sunglasses and soggy Panama hat. He put them on and dangled an unlit cigarette from his lips. "How do I look? Do I look like a twenty-eight-year-old priest?"

"Not even a little," I said.

"That's all right. Father Ted didn't either."

We all breathed easier once we reached the St. Louis city limits and exited the highway. We weren't worried about the city cops pulling us over; they had bigger fish to fry than ticketing traffic violators.

James lived the closest, so we drove to his house first. His family had the nicest digs of all of us. A Fifties ranch in a respectable subdivision. Nothing you'd find on the cover of *Architectural Digest,* but nothing to be ashamed of either. Kevin drew up to the curb a half block from his house and James grabbed his sleeping bag and backpack and eased out the back door.

Dennis reached back and seized James's arm. "Remember what you promised," he said, working to make his voice hard and intimidating—but not quite succeeding.

James stared hard at Dennis, at the hand clutching his arm. His eyes looked wearied and played out. "Let go of my arm."

"We never mention it. Ever."

"I know!" James said with a snarl. "Now get your fucking hand off me!"

Kevin said, "Fellas, we gotta move. Somebody's gonna see me behind the wheel and screw up everything."

"Swear!" Dennis said. "On your mother's life."

"Oh for Christ—" James shook his head. "Fine! I swear."

Dennis turned his eyes on me.

I was almost home. I would have told him literally anything. "Me too," I said.

James jerked his arm away and slammed the door. He hurried past the little manicured lawns toward his house. He never looked back.

We dropped off Dennis next. He was staying with his grandmother about a half mile from James's house. After he got his bags from the cargo compartment, he leaned back into the window and grinned at us. "Let's do this again sometime."

Nobody smiled or said anything.

Then Dennis snorted and thumped the roof of the Jeep and walked off down the cracked, weedy sidewalk.

Kevin and I shared a look of profound relief. I got out of the back seat and slid into the passenger side. "Let's go, before he comes back," I said.

I lived the furthest away—on the other side of the railroad tracks, so to speak. It was a ten-minute drive that we drove in silence. We weren't even in the mood for K-SHE radio. I stared solemnly out the window at the old neighborhood. Everything looked run down and dirty—the used-car lots, the pawn shops, the gone-out-of-business diners and the worn-out four-family housing units. But to me the old place never looked better. Kevin drew up to the curb around the corner from our 1920s bungalow.

We sat there for a moment, watching the street.

"Did you decide what you're gonna do with the Jeep?" I said.

Kevin tapped his thumbs on the steering wheel and gazed absently down the street. "I thought I'd ditch it behind the old shoe factory. It's like a garbage dump back there." He paused. "Don't worry, I'll make sure no one's around."

I nodded.

"Then I'll stick to the back alleys 'til I get home."

"What if someone is around?"

Kevin shrugged. "I'll take it down to the river by the railroad tracks where there's all those rusting barges. Leave it down there somewhere. I don't know. I'll figure it out." A long, slow moment ticked by. "Might be better if you don't know."

I gave a grunt and eased out of the passenger door and glanced up and down the street. I saw only one neighbor, a crabby old coot who hated kids, mowing his tiny patch of front lawn with a reel mower; other than him the street was empty. I went around to the cargo area and got my sleeping bag and duffel and carefully slammed the tailgate closed. "Well good luck," I said. Then I turned and walked toward my house, hoping to God I never saw any of those people ever again.

PART II

HOME

CHAPTER 20

FOR A TIME nothing happened. There were all kinds of wild rumors. Rumors of Father Ted having suffered a nervous breakdown, of him stealing off somewhere to figure things out. That wouldn't be too unusual with young priests who, after all, were put in the very unnatural position of being unable to do something as natural and probably necessary as having sex, or going on a bender now and then, or even questioning the meaning of life. Basically acting like a typical red-blooded American male. It was a wonder more priests didn't wind up missing or locked in the loony bin.

Some folks (middle-aged guys, especially) wondered if Father Ted hadn't gotten tired of being a priest, because, let's face it, they would sure get tired of it pretty quickly. And some of the women wondered if he wasn't off having a torrid love affair with some Jezebel. I never heard anyone speculate about Father Ted having a torrid love affair with the male equivalent of a Jezebel, or of him taking advantage of some poor helpless child. Most people expected he would come crawling back with his tail between his legs by Sunday morning Mass.

I took to riding my bicycle up and down 22nd Street where Mary Beth Franklin lived (wearing my new plaster cast—sure enough, I'd broken my hand) just to see if the Jeep Wagoneer was parked in the driveway. It never was. Once I saw Mary

Beth and her kid sister in their front yard practicing cheers, and she waved to me as I passed, but I was too shy and too ashamed of myself to stop. I didn't exactly have a crush on Mary Beth, but I liked her. At least she was never snotty to me or stuck up like the other cheerleaders. I still remember going to high school parties and trying to be accepted, trying to fit in—which was dumb, because I had no idea how to fit in, and probably wouldn't have wanted to do the things necessary to fit in even if I knew what they were. Anyway, I'd go to these parties and the other teens would be like, *What's he doing here? Who told him about this party? Maybe if we pretend he doesn't exist he'll take the hint and leave.* But there was this one time I showed up to this party where our high school class was building our homecoming float and Mary Beth was there and to my great surprise she came up to me and said hi. We didn't talk much—pretty girls always made my brain shut down—but I always remembered that she made an effort to talk to me when no one else ever would. It's the little things, as they say. And now here was Hillbilly Death lurking on her doorstep, lying in wait for Mary Beth and her poor, unsuspecting family, and it was all my fault.

Well, partly my fault.

I thought about making an anonymous phone call to the police, calling from the phone booth at the Shell station, and telling the cops that they should keep a close eye on the Franklin house.

I could just imagine how well that conversation would go.

Keep an eye on the Franklin house? Why?

Well, some bad men might want to do them harm.

What bad men?

Um. Evil hillbillies.

Yeah? Why would evil hillbillies want to harm the Franklins?

Well, I can't go into that, but you've got to trust this anonymous kid calling from a random pay phone.

Why?

Ummm. Never mind. Click. Buzzzzzzzzz.

Anyway, I could hardly call the cops without giving everything away, and I still couldn't bring myself to do that because that would have taken guts and grit and moral courage and other things I sorely lacked.

So I waved back to Mary Beth and her kid sister and raced on down 22nd Street.

TEN DAYS AFTER we got back from the float trip the metropolitan police found the abandoned Jeep with its smashed bumper and shot-riddled tailgate. After that the rumors really started flying. There was a front-page article in the Sunday *Post-Dispatch,* which, thank God, I didn't have to hand-deliver to my deadbeat customers; those Sunday papers weighed about ten pounds each.

If I live to be a hundred, I'll never forget that front page headline:

SHOT-RIDDLED JEEP DRIVEN
BY MISSING PRIEST FOUND

The headline basically contained the whole story. A reporter interviewed a spokesman for the Archdiocese of St. Louis, but he would say only that everyone was praying that Father Ted would be found unharmed. Nor were the police were commenting, except to say that the Jeep was found near an abandoned shoe factory, and that they were following some unspecified leads. The article didn't say who the Jeep belonged to, just that it was registered to a friend of the missing priest.

My hands trembled as I held the newspaper over my breakfast cereal. My mother came into the kitchen and stared at me, worry lines creasing her brow. "Are you feeling okay? You look white as a sheet." I guess she got a peek at the headline, because she came over and rested her hand on my shoulder and said, "You're worried about Father Ted. Well, the best thing we can do is say a prayer to St. Jude that he's okay. St. Jude and St. Anthony."

Why, I wondered. Were they the patron saints for missing child molesters?

I set down the paper and got to my feet, knocking over a glass of milk. I scrambled to wipe up the spill with a dishrag.

"Let me do that," my mother said. "Why don't you go outside and get some fresh air."

I went and sat on the back porch feeling as jumpy as a cat in a bathhouse. I knew they'd be looking high and low for Father Ted and that they would find the Jeep eventually. I knew I'd be one of the first people they'd want to talk to. At least they would start off talking. After that who knows where things might go?

But it never seemed really real until I saw that headline.

I had to call James. I needed to talk to someone. More importantly, I had to know if any of us had squealed.

When I was finally alone in the house (our only phone hung on the wall in the kitchen) I dialed James's number. His mother answered. We made small talk about how long it had been since I'd visited. I didn't tell her it was because her nerd son now thought he was too cool for me. Finally, she went and got James.

"Yeah?"

It was not a friendly yeah.

I said, "Did you see the newspaper?"

There was a lull. Then James said, "We're not supposed to talk about it." He sounded pissed off for some reason.

"We're not supposed to *tell other people*," I said.

"No, we're not supposed to talk about it—period!"

I couldn't believe he was being a dick about this. I mean, it was kind of important to know where we stood, or if anybody had talked.

Oh well.

"Sorry for bothering you," I said, and I hung up the phone.

JACKS FORK

***

SUMMER EVENTUALLY PASSED. It seemed like the longer we got away with it, the less going to the police was a viable option. Almost like the time limit for coming clean had expired.

Of course I knew that if I didn't go to the police, they would eventually come to me. I wasn't sure how they'd find us, but I *knew* they would. I had prepared myself mentally, going over our story in my mind countless times, reminding myself to say as little as possible, to stick to the story and hope the others would too.

What troubled me most was the possibility that one of them would crack. James, most likely. I could see him panicking and telling the police everything. I could see myself ending up looking like the ringleader, instead of the one who wanted to go to the cops all along.

I could totally see that happening.

"Yes sir, your honor, it was Roy who masterminded the whole operation. The rest of us were mere pawns in his twisted and diabolical scheme."

I pushed away thoughts of the Sikas and what they might do to the Franklins if and when they traced that license plate, or what they might do to me and my family if Mr. Franklin gave us up. Assuming Mr. Franklin even knew who went on that float trip.

Religiously speaking, I wasn't so much worried about what God would do to me as what a court of law would do. I figured God would know the truth, so he'd know Father Ted had it coming and that I was more or less an innocent bystander, just a dumb teenager who succumbed to peer pressure. Maybe God would sentence me to ten years in Purgatory. No hard labor. Ten years…I could do that standing on my head. I mean, I'd still have all of eternity, right?

It was the here and now that I was concerned with—where ten years was still a big freaking deal.

No, it was what I didn't know that worried me. Was it naive of me to think the others wouldn't cut a deal to save their own skins? Was I a fool for not picking up the phone and calling the police, and doing it now, before James or Kevin did? Maybe I could still make a deal where I wouldn't have to serve time. Just probation and community service. Maybe I could still graduate high school. Even go to college.

Of course I'd need a lawyer for that. And my family couldn't afford a lawyer. Only James's family could afford an attorney. And a cheap one at that.

At that very moment, James's cheap lawyer was probably cutting a deal with the state's attorney so that he could graduate high school and attend college. And a few hours after that, a SWAT team would be racing to our house with orders to take me in. Dead or alive.

CHAPTER 21

I WAS STILL sleeping when my mother hollered up the stairs. Someone at the front door wanted to speak to me. I glanced at my alarm clock. It was nine thirty.

Not the way you want to start the day—some unknown person coming to your house to see you first thing in the morning. I got a heavy feeling in the pit of my stomach. For the past couple days my paranoia had been growing like a particularly aggressive tumor, until I saw policemen (and sometimes Sikas) around every corner and in every face.

"Who is it?" I said.

"Just come down here."

There was a tension in Mom's voice, which made the heavy feeling in my stomach feel even heavier. I glanced out my bedroom window. You could access the porch roof from there, and once on the roof shimmy down a post to the porch railing and make your getaway. Or break your neck. I'd done it twice (without breaking my neck) when I'd been grounded and I couldn't take being cooped up inside anymore.

I went to the window and looked out over the backyard. The house did not appear to be surrounded by SWAT teams.

I slipped on some cut-offs and my lucky T-shirt—the yellow one with the guy with the big nose and funny walk that said KEEP ON TRUCKIN'. I went downstairs.

I made it as far as the first landing before I drew up short. Inside the front door stood a burly police officer. He looked about my dad's age, balding with a droopy mustache and bushy eyebrows; something about him gave off an ominous vibe that made me want to turn around and bolt back up the stairs and try the bedroom-window escape route. I studied the shiny pistol on his hip. He held his policeman's cap by the brim at crotch-level like his mother must have taught him.

"Son, when you go to a house to arrest a teenage member of a priest-killing gang, always remove your hat when you enter the front door."

"Yes, Ma."

"It's good manners."

"I'll remember, Ma."

I heard my mother say, "Can't this wait until my husband gets home?"

She was tense all right. Mom was one of those reticent mid-century ladies who let their husbands handle everything that wasn't housekeeping-related. That tension manifested itself in a way that made her appear to be uncooperative, when the fact was, she was just nervous. Jumpy as a trout, you might say.

"I just have a few questions, ma'am."

"Why couldn't they have sent Tim Przybysz?"

"I don't know, ma'am. Who's Tim Przybysz?"

"He's a policeman from our parish."

"Przybysz...Is he a member of the metropolitan police force?"

"The county police."

"Well ma'am, this here is the city."

My mother wrung her hands while she seemed to study the pattern of the carpet. "Well, then, I guess you better come in. But I think we should wait until my husband gets home. Would you like some coffee? I could make a fresh pot. It's no trouble."

"When is your husband expected?"

"He usually comes home for lunch."

The officer glanced at his watch and frowned slightly. "It's only nine thirty, ma'am. I can't sit here drinking coffee for two and a half hours."

"Couldn't Tim Przybysz come by later when my husband's home?"

"He's not a metropolitan police officer, ma'am. Besides, this shouldn't take more than a few minutes."

My mother stared into the distance, her lips were pinched, her face downcast and glum. "Well, if it's only for a few minutes."

They moved into the living room. My mother took a seat at the end of the couch and the police officer settled into our rocking chair. He didn't rock though. I suppose that would have seemed unprofessional. He set his police cap on his lap.

"So they haven't found Father Ted yet?" my mother said.

"No ma'am, we haven't located him just yet."

"So very strange, him just vanishing like that."

The officer nodded, though he'd probably seen a lot stranger things in his day. Naked people screaming on street corners. Hostage situations. Decapitated heads in deep freezers. He removed a notepad and pen from his shirt pocket and flipped to a blank page.

I crept down the steps and went over and sat beside my mother. The policeman leveled his gaze on me. I could feel the full weight of that gaze. It weighed two thousand, two hundred and eighty pounds.

"You're Roy Haas?"

I nodded.

"I'd like to ask you a couple questions, if that's okay."

I knew perfectly well what he was going to ask me.

Why did you murder Father Ted Delaney?

You were the mastermind behind the whole scheme, weren't you?

Was it worth it, that measly ninety-six dollars?

Those kinds of questions.

I gave a noncommittal shrug.

"You were one of the boys who went camping with Father Ted Delaney the last week of July?"

"Um-hm."

"Is that a yes?"

"Yeah."

"When was the last time you saw Father Delaney?"

I glanced at my mother; her eyes were anxiously fixed upon my face. I could tell she was going to be no help at all.

"When he dropped me off."

"When did he drop you off?"

"Friday morning?"

"Is that a question or an answer?"

"Answer?"

The officer frowned. "Exactly what time did he drop you off?"

"Around eleven, I guess. I wasn't really paying attention to what time it was."

"At your home?"

"Huh?"

"Where'd he drop you off?"

"Right up the street."

"Up the street." He scribbled something on his notepad. "And did you see him after that?"

"Father Ted? No sir. How would I?"

"Did he say anything about where he might be going—after he dropped you boys off? What his plans were for the rest of the day? Or the weekend?"

"Not to me."

The officer's face puckered to a scowl. "Think hard. He didn't mention anything? Anything at all?"

I stared fixedly at the ceiling for a moment like I was really thinking hard about his question. Then I slowly shook my head. "Nope. Nothing."

I drew a breath. Almost a sigh of relief. Maybe I wasn't

going to be arrested. Maybe James or Kevin hadn't confessed and cut a deal after all.

Meanwhile the officer studied me. He tapped on the notepad with his pen over and over. "Why didn't Father Delaney drop you off at your house?"

"He did."

"You said he dropped you off down the street."

"Uh-huh. At the corner."

"So again, why didn't he drop you off at your house?"

I shrugged. "Maybe 'cause it's a one-way street?"

The police officer glanced out the living room window. Sure enough, the cars on both sides of the street were facing east.

Finally my mother worked up the courage to say something. "What's the point of all these questions, officer?"

"Well, ma'am, it's quite simple. We got us a missing priest, and as far as we can tell your son and his friends were the last ones to see him. That we know of."

"I know, but...it almost sounds like you suspect the boys of something."

"They're not my friends," I said.

"What?" said the officer.

"They're *not* my friends."

My mother glanced at me, a quizzical look on her face "What do you mean they're not your friends?"

I shifted uneasily on the couch. I don't know why I said that. I guess I was looking for a way to distance myself from the others—if possible. "I mean...James used to be, but we haven't been real friends since eighth grade," I said. "And I hate Kevin's guts. And I don't even know Dennis."

My mother stared blankly. "Why I thought you and James were best friends. What on earth happened?"

I leaned forward on the couch and rubbed my hands on my thighs. "I don't know. I mean...can we talk about it later?"

"Sure, honey. We don't have to talk about it at all if you don't want to. I just thought you boys were—"

My face grew hot. I felt all the built-up tension of the past two weeks well up inside me, ready to burst like an overheated boiler. I guess it sort of did. "He found some other friends, okay?" I cried. "Who cares? He's a dork anyway."

"Oh," my mother said disconcertedly. "Well." She turned back to the police officer. "Maybe we should wait until my husband gets home."

"Yes, ma'am, but, you know, with a thing like this, a missing person, time is of the essence. The more time passes the colder the trail gets."

"But a few hours can't make much difference, can it?"

"It might." The police officer's face turned grave. "There's just one more thing I need to ask Roy, if that's all right."

Here it comes, I thought.

"We got a report about a missing machine operator down where you and your friends were staying."

"Another missing person!" my mother gasped.

"Name of Dwayne Lee Akers. We know that this Akers fella picked up the keys to a vehicle for you boys at the Iron County sheriff's office. Correct?"

I went dead cold. The Sikas must have gotten to Dwayne. They'd made him disappear. And if they'd gotten to Dwayne…

I felt sick. Throw-up sick.

"Well?" the officer said.

"I-I guess so."

"You guess?"

"I mean, yeah."

He paused.

"I'm curious why Father Delaney's keys were at the Iron County Sheriff's Office? And why you asked a random stranger with a long criminal history to pick them up for you?"

I could feel sweat forming on the back of my neck. "Well, you see, this deputy took our keys."

"Interesting. Why did a deputy take your car keys?"

Say as little as possible. That was the plan.

JACKS FORK

If we weren't so stupid we would have known there was an excellent chance the Sikas would track down Dwayne and that Dwayne would "disappear." And then the police would find out that Dwayne had been at the sheriff's office picking up keys for some non-resident teenagers. And once they started looking into that they'd find a trail of big crunchy breadcrumbs leading straight to Kevin.

The next thing you know, we'd all be getting a visit from one of St. Louis's finest.

"We got pulled over and we only had a learner's permit."

"But you were with Father Delaney? Right?"

"He was resting. He wasn't feeling too good so we wanted to let him rest."

My mother gasped again. "What was the matter with Father Ted?"

"So you stole his vehicle?"

"Borrowed it."

"Did you ask permission?"

I shrugged. "Not really."

"So that's stealing."

"It wasn't his vehicle anyway."

"No? Whose was it?"

"It belongs to the Franklins. They always let Father Delaney borrow it."

The officer frowned. "So why'd you and your...companions... *borrow* the vehicle from Father Delaney?"

"We were starving. We wanted to go to the gas station and get something to eat and it was too far to walk."

The officer nodded his head slightly. "Nothing hits the spot like gas station food," he said and paused. "Let's backtrack. Why'd you ask this random stranger to get your keys for you and not Father Delaney?"

"I told you, he wasn't feeling good. He would've had to walk all the way into town to get the keys."

"What do you mean not feeling well? What was wrong with

him?"

"I don't know. He just said he wasn't feeling good and was gonna get some rest."

The police officer studied me. "Did you pay this fella to get your keys?"

I nodded.

"How much?"

"I don't remember exactly."

"About how much?"

"Fifty bucks?"

"That's a heck of a lot of money. Where'd you kids get fifty bucks?"

"I—we pooled our money."

There was a silence.

"So tell me, what did Father Delaney think of your shenanigans?"

"We never told him. He never found out."

"He was still *resting* when you got back?"

I nodded.

The silence ticked by. We studied each other across the coffee table for a moment.

"That's quite a story," the officer said.

"It's the truth."

"Uh-huh." The officer removed a handkerchief from his trouser pocket and dabbed at his sweaty forehead. His gaze shifted to my mother and he cleared his throat. "Father Delaney's been missing two weeks now. And the man your son paid to get their keys back is also missing. But one thing that ain't missing is the Jeep. We found that not too far from here. Riddled with bullet holes."

"I saw that in the paper," my mom said. She shivered slightly. "Just horrible. I am so worried about Father Delaney."

I couldn't stop thinking about Dwayne. I could just imagine them Sikas doing all kinds of sick and twisted things to him until he gave up our names. Only…he didn't know our names.

Not our last names, anyway.

But the cops knew our names. They knew Kevin's name from his learning permit.

That must have been how they found me. They found Kevin and that bastard must have given up the rest of us...

But how *much* did he tell them?

"He's not even listening," the police officer said. The angry tug in his voice snapped me back to the moment.

"Yes I am."

"Just one more thing," the officer said. "There's one thing I can't quite figure. We had a report of another individual from Iron County, a well-known car thief." He paused a moment to let that sink in. I could hear the old antique clock ticking away on the mantle. The neighbor's beagles were barking as a garbage truck rolled down the alley. Up on Grand Street, an emergency vehicle wailed. There was a lot going on this morning. The officer continued, "This fella was banged up pretty good after his vehicle was struck by an incendiary device and slammed into a utility pole and went over the side of a cliff. Last I heard he was barely holding on." The officer's eyes locked on mine. "They recovered fingerprints from some of them glass fragments."

My mother's eyes were wide as saucers.

"Now here's the funny part. Those prints belonged to the missing machine operator I was telling you about. The fella you paid to get your keys." He paused. "Quite a coincidence, wouldn't you say?"

The officer studied me closely for a moment. He narrowed his eyes a little. "You may as well tell me the truth, son. The more stories you tell the harder it's gonna be..."

"I am telling the truth!" I cried.

At that my mother said, "I don't think I'm comfortable with these questions...at least until my husband gets home."

This time the police officer ignored her. He must have felt he was getting close.

"The other boys weren't so reluctant to talk," he said. "In the long run, they'll be glad they did."

They talked? They confessed? Then why hadn't he arrested me already?

Or was this cop full of shit? Cops weren't allowed to lie, were they? It was against the law, wasn't it? Against the cop's rule book?

Did they even have a rule book?

The police officer gave me what was undoubtedly his most intimidating look. "Now do you want to tell me what really happened down there, Roy?"

My mother stood. "I think that's enough, officer."

The police officer frowned. I could tell my mother was starting to get on his nerves. He slipped the notepad into his shirt pocket, then he let out a long deep breath and got to his feet with a groan.

I swallowed hard and steadied myself for whatever came next. I could almost feel the handcuffs biting into my wrists.

"Of course, ma'am," the police officer said. He sniffed and moved heavily toward the door. At the door he hesitated. "Oh, just one more thing. When you were running around in that Jeep, did you notice any bullet holes or dents in the rear end?"

"No sir."

He nodded. "Uh-huh."

The police officer went out onto the front porch. I still wasn't sure that he wasn't going to cuff me and drag me out to his car. On the porch he turned to my mother standing beside him and smiled broadly and thanked her for her cooperation. He handed her his card and said he would be in touch.

After the police officer drove off, my mother and I stood on the porch a long time not saying anything. I must have been in a state of semi-shock, still trying to figure out what the hell just happened.

My mother gazed into the distance and said, "I wish your father had been here."

Another long moment elapsed, then she turned to me, a strained, almost haunted look on her face. "Roy, why didn't you tell us about this?"

"About what?"

"All of it! About the police taking the keys to your vehicle! About Father Ted getting sick!"

I shrugged. "I guess I didn't want to worry you."

"It's my job to worry!"

I nodded slightly and said, "Then I guess it's my job to give you things to worry about."

I went down the steps and hopped on my bicycle and I took off across the yard. Then I turned down our street, racing as fast as I could to the nearest phone.

CHAPTER 22

AFTER THE POLICE officer left our house, I raced my ten-speed to the 7-Eleven and called James from the outdoor pay phone. This time he didn't scold me for calling. In fact, he said he was about to call me. A city cop had been to see him, too. The way he told it, his interview sounded a lot like mine.

We talked about the cops finding the bullet-riddled Jeep and how the Sikas had the Jeep's license plates so they were bound to show up on the Franklin's doorstep any day now. For me, things had taken on a greater urgency. "We gotta do something," I said. "Send the Franklins an anonymous note or something."

"You think I haven't thought of that?" James said. "Imagine getting an anonymous note saying some country psychopaths might be coming to kill you and your family...what are you gonna think?"

"I don't know what I'd think! But we gotta do something! We could say it has something to do with Father Ted."

"That's as good as saying we killed him."

"Quit saying *we* killed him! *Dennis* killed him."

"We helped cover it up. You know what they say, 'The cover-up is worse than the crime.'"

I'd never heard that before. I wanted to say, *I told you so. From the beginning I told you this would happen*! But besides a fleeting feeling of vindication, what would be the point in rubbing his nose in it?

The line was quiet for a long time. I thought maybe he'd hung up.

"You still there?"

"Yeah."

"So did the cops say anything about Akers?"

"Who's Akers?"

I let out a loud, exasperated sigh. "The guy who helped us! Who got shot in the leg?"

"Oh. They know he got the keys for us."

I nodded. "What did you say?"

"I said we paid him fifty bucks to get the keys back and that was it. We never saw him again." He told me to hang on and said something to someone. A moment later he came back on the phone. "Why what'd you say?"

"The same. They asked me why Father Ted didn't get the keys."

"And?"

"Like we said. He was sick. Resting." I waited. "The police said Dwayne's missing."

"Yeah, them hillbillies probably carved him up and fed him to their dogs."

There was a long, tense silence on the line as we thought about what this could mean for us. Our likely fate as puppy chow.

James said, "You think he gave us up before they...?"

"All he knew was we were some kids from St. Louis. I never told him my name. Any of our names."

"You sure about that?"

All of the sudden I wasn't so sure. "Pretty sure."

There was a deep sigh of relief on the other end of the line. I leaned on the pay phone, feeling the sweat running down my back. "Have you talked with the others?"

"Not to Kevin...and Dennis has disappeared."

"What do you mean?"

"I mean he's not at his grandmother's anymore. Said she doesn't know where he is. That's actually not all that unusual."

"You don't think—?"

"I have no idea."

Another long slow moment went by. Dennis was probably fine. He was likely hiding out somewhere. A guy like that was probably real hard to find if he wanted to be.

I said, "So you think Kevin ratted us out?"

"Of course he did. They had his name from the learner's permit. I just wonder how much he told them."

"He probably made himself look super-innocent."

There was a long pause, then James said, "So you haven't heard anything about the Franklins?"

"As far as I know, they're okay," I said. "Maybe getting Dwayne was enough. Maybe they'll leave them alone."

"Yeah, maybe," James said. "I sure hope so."

I WAS FREAKED OUT for a long time after that, waiting for a gang of crazed rednecks to pull up in a white van some late afternoon while I was shuffling along the railroad tracks on my way home from school. Toss me into the back of their van and that would be it. No witnesses. Like Father Ted, I'd have vanished off the face of the earth.

Like Dwayne.

Like Dennis.

Any day I expected to hear that something terrible had happened to the Franklins. But did I go to the cops? I thought about it. I thought about it every night while I tossed and turned in bed, but in the end I did nothing.

Meanwhile I expected to be arrested any day. Hurled into a crowded cell with rapists and murderers...while the walls closed in.

But neither of these things happened. Don't ask me why.

A few weeks after school started I had mostly put all that dead-priest business behind me. I had stopped jumping at shadows, anyway. Sometimes I would see James in the halls at school, but we didn't say much. He had his new friends and I had my cheap Gibson LG-O guitar that I was learning to play. I'd quit the stupid paper route and gotten a job at Ridel's Restaurant as a busboy and that kept me busy evenings and weekends and I actually made a few dollars.

Kevin transferred to one of the public schools, where they probably had special classes for sadistic bullies and snitches. I saw him around town once or twice, but I never spoke to him again, which is how I preferred it. I never saw Dennis again.

One evening after dinner I overheard my mom and dad talking quietly in the kitchen. They were talking about the Franklins, so I couldn't help eavesdropping. Nick Franklin had told my dad that two strangers had showed up at his house claiming to be private investigators and wanted to know if he'd taken his Jeep to Iron County, Missouri about a month and a half ago. Mr. Franklin told them, no, that that priest who had gone missing had borrowed it, that he always borrowed the Jeep for a few weeks in the summer. Nick said he didn't know what private investigators looked like, but that these two guys looked more like drug dealers and had about eight teeth and forty jailhouse tattoos between them, so unless the private investigation business had fallen on real hard times, something fishy was going on.

They also wanted to know who the priest had taken with him on the camping trip. Mr. Franklin told them he didn't know. They asked him again who the kids were, sounding less and less courteous, but Mr. Franklin repeated that he had no idea, possibly some kids from the parish. Then one of the so-called PIs asked why he was protecting the boys? And Mr. Franklin got his back up and said he wasn't protecting anybody, but even if he did know he wouldn't feel comfortable telling strangers. He told them to ask the police. They probably knew.

The men gave him a hard look, but they left without incident. Mr. Franklin said he double-bolted the door and ran down his basement and retrieved his old service revolver. The whole ordeal left him feeling on edge.

Mr. Franklin said he knew that I had been one of the boys, but there was no way he was going to tell those guys that. He said those men creeped the hell out of him.

That could be why I'm still here today.

EPILOGUE

CHAPTER 23

OUR FORTIETH GRADE-SCHOOL class reunion was held at a seedy little golf course in South County that was co-owned by one of our classmates, a guy named Mike Soto. I had attended only one of our previous reunions, mainly because I had moved around a lot and hadn't known about them. I never went to any of my high school reunions because I hadn't had any friends to speak of in high school, so I never saw the point. I guess I still held a grudge against my high school classmates. That's what happens when you last see your contemporaries at age eighteen, in their sadistic and snobbish prime. And even though four decades had passed, and we'd all grown up, married, raised families, divorced, and turned into boring, respectable, tax-paying citizens—as far as I was concerned they were still the same vicious Hitler Youth that gave me wedgies in P.E. class.

I know it's silly to hold a grudge like that, but I don't make the rules.

Grade school was different. We were just kids. Innocent and clueless, for the most part. Too young to be cliquey and cool. I had a few fond memories of grade school and I was looking forward to seeing my classmates. I wondered if Kevin and James would show up, and if so, if we would have the nerve to talk about what happened all those summers ago.

In all that time I had never mentioned Father Ted's name—

not even to my wife (now ex-wife). I'd been tempted...lots of times. But with him still lying out there in that gully next to a southeast Missouri crop field, I couldn't bring myself to do it. As far as I knew there was no statute of limitations for murder.

The reunion had been underway for about two hours when I got there. Mary Beth Franklin—now Mary Beth Franklin-Hopper—welcomed me at the reception table with a toothy grin and a warm hug (the first time I had ever touched, let alone hugged her in my life!). She gave me a name tag with my second-grade yearbook photo in black-and-white pasted on it. Mary Beth seemed to be holding up better than most of our classmates. Maybe it was all that cheerleading. She looked a lot like her mother used to look back in the Seventies—which was the last time I'd seen her mother—so that now, in my mind's eye anyway, they were multi-generational twins. It was a weird feeling. I really wanted to tell Mary Beth that I was glad nobody ever killed her and her family, but I didn't because that would have freaked her out, and I was trying really hard not to do that.

We chatted a minute over the loud mid-1970s themed music—which was probably a half minute more than we'd ever talked before—then she went to check someone else in and I went over to say hi to Kenny Mank, the guy who had put the reunion together. Kenny was a classmate I had never particularly liked nor disliked. He didn't look too bad, either. Bald and a little heavier, but somehow it suited him. He'd always had the personality of a persnickety old man, even in grade school. Kenny said that eighteen of us had shown up tonight, fourteen of them girls—well, middle-aged women, now. I glanced around the room, only recognizing a handful of people, struggling to find traces of pubescent faces concealed among the wrinkles and loose flesh and thick layers of makeup. Most of them, the last time I had seen them, were fourteen years old. Six or so years from their prime. Their whole lives ahead of them.

I felt like a ghoul, but I went ahead and asked Kenny to

update me on who had passed away. Without hesitation, he ticked off a disturbingly long list of names. So I wasn't the only ghoul. *Let's see, there was Tom Ray. Jimmy Boyle. Jerry Freivogal. Chip Rust. Carl Paule...*The deceased were all guys, the ones you might have guessed would be dead, if you had to guess. The ones from the poor, dysfunctional homes who dropped out of high school and spent most of their time either *in* bars or *behind* bars. With one exception. Toby Rogers. The popular son of a bitch who had come up with my lousy grade-school nickname. Kenny said he was killed in a workplace accident in Tennessee. There was no other information. (I can't say I took the news very hard.) The other deaths were no accidents. There were likely more deceased classmates—at least a couple of women gone from various cancers—but no one knew for sure. There had been sixty-five of us in our Baby Boomer class, give or take. Two-thirds of them seemed to have just stepped off the face of the earth.

I thought I recognized a gaunt middle-aged guy at the bar chatting up the young barmaid. I asked Kenny who it was, and sure enough, it was my one-time best friend James, though now with considerably less hair, a short gray beard, and, oddly enough, no spectacles. I told Kenny I'd talk at him later and strode over to the bar and stuck out my hand. James didn't look surprised to see me, nor did he seem particularly glad, but we shook hands and he gave me an amiable clap on the shoulder. I bought a round of drinks and we did the standard catching-up. It's strange and a little sad how fast you can catch up. How quickly you can sum up forty years of life. It only takes about four minutes, tops. And that's if you include some of the boring stuff that nobody cares about.

James was retired Air Force, a former fighter pilot, which surprised the hell out of me. I would have figured him for an actuary or insurance agent maybe. Something dull and lucrative. He'd flown missions in Kosovo and received several decorations and commendations for blowing shit up. He was now principal at a Catholic school for low-income students and was getting ready to retire from that too. He had two kids—grown now—and two grandchildren. His wife passed away seven years ago. I didn't ask for details and he didn't volunteer any.

At least that's what I think he said. By the time the night was over I'd heard so many life stories that they all ran together. But the recurring theme was that we were all grandparents, easing into retirement, some divorced, a few widowed, all glad that we weren't among the roll call of dead, and that eighth-grade graduation seemed like it was only yesterday, and *aw shit, it's good to see you, let's have another drink. Sorry, I'd like to, but it's late and I gotta long drive, but it sure was good seeing you...*

James said, "How about you? What've you been up to? Kids? Still playing music?"

I told him about my daughter out in Omaha, a legal secretary for a slip-and-fall firm currently working on marriage number two. She had a couple of stepdaughters who didn't completely hate her. I got along with her husband okay. I usually drove out at Christmas for a day or two. Other than that, I was still delivering mail for the postal service, still playing guitar, and running the open mic at the local coffeehouse Thursday nights. That was pretty much the extent of it. (I saw no point in mentioning my colon cancer, since it was supposedly in remission.) Not where I thought I'd be at this stage of life, but I wasn't complaining. Anyway, I don't think James was even listening. He seemed bored. I guess everything is boring after you've wiped out entire villages in a B-2 bomber.

After we ran out of easy things to say and the talk turned strained and awkward, I decided to throw caution to the wind and asked James if he ever heard from his cousin. He gave me a look as if to say, *Really? You really want to go there?*

I gave him a look back that said, Why not? There may not be a next time.

James's face puckered into a scowl and he stared off into the distance in a stony silence. Then he turned and strode down to the far end of the bar.

Wow, I really stuck my foot in it this time, I thought.

Then, to my surprise, he motioned for me to join him. I went down and took a seat on the last barstool.

Dennis, he said, had OD'd on something, probably heroin, back in the late Eighties, which came as a surprise to exactly no one. Still, I found the news aggravating.

"So we risked our lives...and all those people died...just so he could kill himself ten years later."

"Don't be too hard on him. The poor guy suffered a lot of trauma."

I wondered about that. He certainly caused a lot of trauma.

We fell silent again. I finally broke the silence by noting that Kevin hadn't made an appearance. James said he'd heard that Kevin was a corrections officer in Florida, which seemed like the perfect job for him, riding a horse and toting a shotgun through the swamps in the blazing heat, bullying prisoners, and in general enjoying life. (Later another classmate told me he ran a fishing boat off the coast of Gulf Shores, Alabama, so who really knows?) I tried to smooth things over by buying us another round of drinks. After that we stepped outside onto the deck, away from the sounds of the Steve Miller Band and Fleetwood Mac and Supertramp. We leaned on the deck railing overlooking the sunburnt fairway and stiffly nursed our drinks. Drunken, middle-aged, white folks' laughter and Foreigner's "Hot Blooded" drifted through the open windows. In the gathering dusk, a foursome weaved their golf carts in from the eighteenth hole.

I did learn one new thing. While we were out on the deck making stiff, way-too-sober conversation, James mentioned that twenty years ago another boy had come forward with an accusation against Father Ted. It had apparently been in the newspapers at the time, though I hadn't heard anything about it. Twenty years ago I was living with a woman in Moberly,

Kansas and had lost touch with what was happening back home. James said the accuser refused to settle and eventually won two million bucks from the archdiocese.

"They almost always settle these things before a lawsuit is filed, so who knows how many others there were," he said.

For a while we watched the teenage staff hosing off the golf carts and, more to the point, each other. We couldn't hear what they were saying over the roar of the cicadas and Jethro Tull's "Too Old to Rock and Roll, Too Young to Die;" no doubt the same things sixteen-year-old boys and girls have always said to each other on warm summer nights.

James said, "To think, if he hadn't OD'd, Dennis could have gotten himself a cheap lawyer and been a multi-millionaire by now."

"I don't know," I said. "I kind of think there are statutes of limitations on things like that." I wasn't really sure how any of that worked. Maybe I'd ask my daughter next Christmas.

The ninth hole green had slipped into full shadow. I was starting to feel a bit tipsy, a bit nostalgic, a bit melancholy, and dare I say, even a bit cheerful. After a long silence, I turned back to James. "So, for real," I said. "Did you ever talk about it...to anyone?"

James took a sip of his scotch and soda. "About Father Ted?" He shook his head. Then he grew thoughtful. "I almost told my sister...I'd be over at her place during the holidays and I'd have a few too many scotch-and-sodas. But something always stopped me. Maybe it was that promise we made. I've always been a stickler for keeping promises." His eyes went distant. "I'm glad I didn't. She didn't need to know that shit. It would've just made her feel bad." He paused and looked me squarely in the eye. "How about you?"

I pressed my lips into a fine line and shook my head. "I went through a period, in my twenties, early thirties, where I forgot it ever happened. Scariest, most traumatic thing that ever happened to me and I completely blocked it out."

James nodded for a minute.

Then I said, "When the Boston sex-abuse story was all over the news...that's when it all came rushing back. But by then it seemed like ancient history." I took a sip of my beer. "Hell, even then I wasn't sure we couldn't be arrested. There's no statute of limitations for murder. Or whatever it was."

James grunted and we grew silent. After a while, he gazed out over the golf course and said he thought he'd call it a night. Maybe slip out the back way so he didn't have to say a lot of goodbyes. "I hate goodbyes," he said.

I said I might hang around a while longer. Maybe find out the fates of a few more dead classmates.

James gave me a forced smile, then he downed the last of his scotch and set his empty glass on the railing. "It was good seeing you," he said rather listlessly, and put out his hand.

"You too," I said. As we shook hands, I had the feeling it would be the last time we spoke, and I was okay with that.

Only I couldn't let him go just yet. There was one last bit of unfinished business. As he started toward the stairs, I called out after him. "So...do you think we did the right thing?"

It stopped him, and he slowly turned to face me. I couldn't read his expression—I never could—but he didn't seem particularly annoyed at my question. After a long moment he said, "Shit, Roy, there wasn't no right thing."

I studied his face. "You believe that?"

"Right, wrong, what the hell's the difference what you call it? We did what we had to do."

I nodded gravely. "Anyway, we were just kids," I said. "What the hell did we know?"

"We knew enough to get away with it," he said. "We knew that much."

Yeah. I guess we did.

He gazed around absently, anxious to take his leave. "Well, you take it easy," he said.

I raised my beer to him. "Maybe I'll see you at the fiftieth."

James gave me a cryptic half grin. "I don't think so. After forty these things get too morbid for me. Too many ghosts."

"Yeah." I nodded my head slowly. Those were my thoughts exactly.

He went down the back steps, past the line of empty golf carts, and around the corner of the clubhouse leaving me alone out on the deck overlooking Mike Soto's shabby golf course.

I picked up James's empty glass and I went back inside. The reunion was starting to wind down. It was way past most of our bedtimes. Bored husbands were pressing their wives to take their leave. Two old classmates hugged drunkenly near the exit, saying their teary goodbyes. I spied Kenny Mank over by the picked-over hors d'oeuvres table; I thought I'd walk over and give him an update for his dead-classmate list. And maybe after that I'd go over and talk to Mary Beth again. And I would have, too, except she was already gone.

CHRIS ORLET is the author of several published crime/noir novels, including *Jacks Fork*, *So Many Things to Bury* and *A Taste of Shotgun* (Down & Out Books), and *In the Pines* (New Pulp Press). He is a former Peace Corps volunteer, and is currently a college instructor in the Illinois state prison system.

On the following pages are a few
more great titles from the
Down & Out Books publishing family.

For a complete list of books and to
sign up for our newsletter,
go to DownAndOutBooks.com.

Calypso Blue
A Len Buonfiglio/Caribbean Mystery
Brian Silverman

Down & Out Books
June 2025
978-1-64396-394-5

Bar owner and ex-New Yorker Len Buonfiglio, a hero in his hometown, flees his family and the city for what he hopes is a quieter, idyllic life in the tropics. But when Lord Ram, a world-renowned Calypso performer dies, Len is called in to quiet damning rumors about the man's death.

In his search for the truth about Lord Ram and dealing with the very dangerous mess Maurizio has brought with him, Len soon learns that even on a sunny tropical paradise there is no escape from darkness.

The Gorgon of Los Feliz
Nolan Knight

Down & Out Books
July 2025
978-1-64396-397-6

The Gorgon of Los Feliz is Cameron Kilbride, a bisexual female in her early twenties, newly evicted, hustling a living by rolling tourists on the fringe of Hollywood, stealing cars—*anything* to get by. Enter the affluent Stevensons; Richard and Mauve have lost track of their troubled daughter, Tiffany, and fear she has fallen back into pills, last seen on tour across America with a psychedelic rock band. Desperate to reel her back home, they employ Cam, who makes it her life's mission to find Tiffany for a handsome reward. When she finds their daughter, things soon go haywire, forcing her to steal the girl's identity to bilk her inheritance; however, once she procures this troubled life, the sordid characters in Tiff's world begin to haunt her every step.

Silent Killer
Tracy Burnett & Ross Weiland

Down & Out Books
August 2025
978-1-64396-413-3

Gordon Stone is an investigator assigned to the FBI Joint Terrorism Task Force. He's given an insignificant case—a charity scam out of Africa—and ordered to close it.

For Gordon, it's not that simple. Gordon has high-functioning autism. He's socially awkward, but blessed with a superpower—extraordinary focus and attention to detail. That superpower allows Gordon to piece together a disparate puzzle: a Hunter-Killer drone; an illicit drug shipment; a Special Forces operation gone wrong; and illegal immigration linked to 9/11.

When these pieces align, national security is at risk and hundreds of lives hang in the balance.

Dead in the Quarter
A Jonathan Brooks Novel
A.C. Frieden

Down & Out Books
September 2025
978-1-64396-415-7

After a celebratory dinner at a Mississippi riverfront restaurant marking his promotion to named partner, attorney Tod Rochon heads home to the French Quarter. In the dead of night, managing partner Jonathan Brooks gets a call from the police: Tod has been found gravely injured. Soon after Jonathan reaches the E.R., Tod is gone.

Driven by suspicion and grief, Jonathan starts digging. But the deeper he goes, the more unsettling the picture becomes—not just outside the firm, but within.

www.ingramcontent.com/pod-product-compliance
Lightning Source LLC
Chambersburg PA
CBHW031146020426
42333CB00013B/540

* 9 7 8 1 6 4 3 9 6 4 1 6 4 *